Prophetic JOURNEY

~ RUTH MANGIACAPRE

To Contact the Author:
www.impactministrytriad.com
Ruthmangia417@gmail.com

To Contact the Publisher:
South Main Media ™, A Creative Company of Mindwatering
520 South Main Street, Wake Forest, North Carolina 27587
www.southmainmedia.com, www.mindwatering.com
contact@southmainmedia.com

International Standard Book Number: 978-0-9909737-2-0
First Edition - Paperback & eBook

Cover design & book layout by South Main Media.

SOUTH MAIN MEDIA™

Changing the Culture
DESIGN HOUSE
RECORDING STUDIO
BOOK PUBLISHING

WWW.SOUTHMAINMEDIA.COM

Endorsements

It is a pleasure to write this endorsement for Ruth Mangiacapre. Let me start off by saying that integrity is everything when it comes to ministry. Ruth is a devoted mother, wife, grandmother; and most of all, a dedicated Christian. Ruth has been a blessing to New Day the Church at High Point for many years. She teaches, imparts, and truly has a desire to see people advance in the calling that is on their lives. Her chief characteristic is integrity as a prophet of the Lord. I would recommend her for ministry at the highest level. Ruth lives what she teaches and knows how to impart life to the hearer. In all the years of knowing Ruth, I have never heard a bad report about her. She is always striving to learn more, to know more, so she can bring more illumination to those to whom she is training or ministering. As her Pastor, I am so blessed to have her not only be in our church, but to be part of the pastoral leadership staff. Ruth is also part of our Presbytery council and is an instructor in the 5Runner School of Ministry. Ruth is a gemstone given to the body of Christ, and I recommend her with the highest honors.

APOSTLE MIKE SIRIANNI
Senior Pastor of New Day the Church at High Point

As part of Ruth's spiritual oversight, I can say that I completely trust her ability to hear the voice of God. She is one who loves to live in His presence and knows how to minister from there, demonstrating the Kingdom of God by healing the sick, bringing restoration to broken places, and hope to those without. A woman of boldness and courage, Ruth teaches with clarity, trains, activates and imparts to all who yearn to hear God's voice and find their destiny. She is compassionate and sensitive as her passion for the King of Glory is shared with all who desire to know more about Him and His ways. Ruth is flexible and refuses to put God in a box, wanting to do things His way rather than the way of tradition or man's expectations. For all these reasons and more, I highly recommend Ruth Mangiacapre's ministry.

THE LATE GARY BROOKS
In His Image Ministries

Ruth Mangiacapre is an amazing seer/prophet that has heavenly experiences on a regular basis. Her teaching and preaching is accompanied with a clear authority that often brings demonstrations of Holy Spirit with power. I believe Ruth is one of many that God is using in this day to lift the Body of Christ to a place of hearing and seeing in the Spirit. This generation will go far beyond the normative mindset of the day to demonstrate Kingdom Power. I highly recommend the ministry of Ruth Mangiacapre.

JEFF JANSEN
Founder Global Fire Ministries

Ruth Mangiacapre is a prophetic minister who flows in a strong teaching anointing. With over 12 years of ministry experience in both pastoral ministry and prophetic counseling, Ruth is anointed to empower believers and see them activated in their unique gifts and callings. I have known Ruth personally for several years and can attest to her purity of heart and character before God. She will be a great blessing to your church.

MATT SORGER
Matt Sorger Ministries

There are many favorable words that could describe Ruth Mangiacapre, but perhaps the best description one could give is, "friend of God". Ruth's ministry is characterized by a prophetic anointing that carries an authority to lift individuals and churches to a greater level of purpose and destiny. As a gifted prophet who functions within a strong local church community, her experience and anointing are extremely valuable to local churches in practically expressing a Kingdom culture. It is for these reasons and many more that Ruth Mangiacapre carries my highest recommendation.

ABNER SUAREZ
For Such a Time as This

THANK YOU

A very special thank you to Brent and Renna Turf; Mama Frances; my administrator, Donna Key; my New Day Church family; all my partners and intercessors; my Long Island girlfriends; every pastor that has ever opened up their pulpit to me; and all the many students who have gone through the New Day the Church at High Point's 5 Runner School of the Prophets.

I would also like to express my gratitude to some amazing ladies who proof-read and offered their love in doing so; Drenda Lalor, Conny Hubbard, Sandi Jenkins, and Heidi Walker.

Your love, words of affirmation, and encouragement have inspired, and continue to inspire me to serve God wholeheartedly, and to love His people. Each one of you are so gifted and loved!

Thank you!

$\mathcal{D}$EDICATION

To my husband, Andy, who always encouraged me to be who I was created to be, without reservations, who loves me unconditionally, and guides me with his gentle wisdom. After all these years, you are still my best friend.

To Andrew and Amanda, Dana, Jerod, Jude, and James – my greatest joy is still being a mom and nana. You make it so easy to keep my priorities straight. I love you all so very much!

To my mentors and friends – the late Gary Brooks, Martha and Jerry Hester, Joni Ames, Abner Suarez, Mike and Debbie Sirianni, Mike and Sharon Adams and, oh, so many more to count. You set such standards for me in ministry and empowered me to become all that God intended me to be. I cherish you all for the role models that each of you are. Thank you for the humility and integrity you all displayed.

To the King of Glory, the Savior of the world, my very best Friend and Counselor – may my life speak not only with words, but in love and compassion to represent you well. I long to leave a legacy that will empower others to live their dreams!

My Prophetic Journey

This book is written to those who desire mentoring, encouragement, and wisdom in the development of their prophetic calling. It is specifically written not only to inspire you, but to bring understanding and clarity to your individual, unique prophetic journey. I, along with all of Heaven, cheer you on!

TABLE OF CONTENTS

FOREWORD

These are amazing times in which we live. Those who are alive on the earth have the privilege of playing a significant roll in training and equipping the saints. Things are moving at warp speed, and there seems to be no limit to how fast God is moving to bring forth the Third Great Awakening in its fullness. Before the foundation of the earth, God set forth His will to establish certain individuals who would be alive to continue the work that has been in progress over the centuries. These anointed vessels would have to be mature and sensitive, and have a track record of bearing fruit geared towards the apostolic reformation.

It's an honor and a privilege to not only write this forward for Ruth Mangiacapre, but it's also an honor to serve alongside her, and to have her as a part of the New Day leadership team. Ruth serves as instructor in the School of the Prophets at 5Runner School of Ministry at New Day the Church at High Point, and as an advisor for New Day's Presbytery council. She is also in full-time itinerant ministry.

Ruth is a mature and joyful Servant of the Lord who takes her calling very seriously. She has continually asserted herself in Biblical training and spiritual enrichment, and continually surrounds herself with leaders in her field that challenge her for the greater. Through the years of knowing Ruth, she has trained many sons and daughters who have gone out and advanced the kingdom of Heaven on earth. Such a mandate can only be fulfilled by skilled workers, like Ruth, who are willing to be tested by every word that proceeds from their lips. Ruth is a passionate and intentional forerunner who pulls down revelation, which opens the door for others to recognize their own calling to comfortably step out into uncharted territory.

As her Pastor, I highly recommend Ruth and her teachings. I can proudly vouch for her character, integrity, and track record of being a humble minister and fearless leader. What a gift to the Body of Christ! Well done, Ruth!

APOSTLE MIKE SIRIANNI
Senior Pastor of New Day the Church at High Point

THE MOUTHPIECE

©2007 RUTH MANGIACAPRE

There are times I've lost my voice in the sea of religion,
Accusation and discouragement.
So I abandoned my message for another time and place.
Hoping it would re-emerge in some other mouthpiece
More confident than I.
Yet the fire from heaven shut up in these frail bones
Became more inflamed
As I sat immobile at the door of the Royal One
Who shed Grace through the cracks of my broken vessel.
Positioning oneself for usefulness is not the impossible task
My thoughts had embellished.
I, too, had a Samaritan tale,
A divine encounter with Truth Himself.
My whispers are gaining more strength.
Octaves increasing in effectiveness.
As my eyes lock into your piercing gaze.
This story must be pronounced!
It cannot lie silent through another season.
For you are the message!
These lips decree what my eyes have seen.
Simply, yet profoundly wonderful!

All fear is removed as love pulls back the layers of falsehood.

Truth is what it is. It never changes.

Truth is He!

He overshadows our inadequacies by the mere glimpse of His Glory!

Thus we proclaim.

No longer an empty mouthpiece void of power and passion,

A rote expression we heard on recycle.

Now fresh manna to feed the impoverished –

Thus the birth of the pure prophetic voice!

ꙮNTRODUCTION

The beginning of my prophetic journey began in 1981. I was saved at an *Amway* convention and knew very little of what a true Christian lifestyle entailed. I was unschooled in doctrine, religion, and the charismatic culture. Relationship with God became my highest priority.

Being abandoned by my father at the age of eight created a "black hole" in my heart. I spent much of my childhood depressed, anxious, and yearning for daddy's presence. In time, I would discover that my heavenly Father's presence was the seed for an enduring prophetic lifestyle. Lasting security was found only in His loving arms.

> ROMANS 8:38 (NKJV) "FOR I AM PERSUADED THAT NEITHER DEATH NOR LIFE, NOR ANGELS NOR PRINCIPALITIES NOR POWERS, NOR THINGS PRESENT NOR THINGS TO COME, NOR HEIGHT NOR DEPTH, NOR ANY OTHER CREATED THING, SHALL BE ABLE TO SEPARATE US FROM THE LOVE OF GOD WHICH IS IN CHRIST JESUS OUR LORD."

Many are enamored by the gifts of the Spirit. Embracing the prophetic as a lifestyle begins and ends with revelation of God's love, goodness, and mercy. For it is in this place that we rest securely in grace. Our motives are tried, hearts are revealed and ultimately healed.

I invite you to come. Let us fasten our seat belts and fly into the realms of His Spirit with joy and delight. Revelation unfolds as simplicity is maintained. My prayer is that the reader turns the pages of this book and discovers grace for the race, boldness to "become," and childlike faith to soar into his or her own prophetic destiny!

$\mathcal{B}$EGINNINGS

My prophetic journey began very early on. **Psalm 139:16 (AMP)** states,

> "YOUR EYES SAW MY UNFORMED SUBSTANCE, AND IN YOUR BOOK ALL THE DAYS (OF MY LIFE) WERE WRITTEN BEFORE EVER THEY TOOK SHAPE, WHEN AS YET THERE WAS NONE OF THEM."

Long before I was "born again," I was perceptive to my surroundings. My mother always said I was emotional. Teachers said I daydreamed, and doctors labeled me as "emotional, neurotic, and flighty." Sensitivity was my enemy in an unstable home environment.

I have only recently been able to embrace my "total" self with spiritual understanding. I was an emerging prophet! If only someone would have recognized my "sensitivity" or mentored me along the way, extending grace to my learning, I may have been able to avoid so many pitfalls. But God was birthing in me an understanding of the painstaking process of "becoming."

From an early age I always just "knew" things. I "knew" when my father was about to leave again and again. I "knew" when and what my Italian speaking grandparents were talking about even though I never learned the language. I "knew" what time it was without ever looking at a clock. I "knew" when someone was deeply suffering because I perceptively experienced their internal pain. This can be quite grueling to a child who had no one to talk to.

My mother worked two jobs. As the oldest daughter, I learned responsibility from an early age. I did not want to care for my younger siblings; instead, I just wanted to imagine, daydream, and pen simple poetry. This resentment of my lost identity made me feel lonely and misunderstood. I longed for significance and purpose. I even struggled adapting as a student. Coloring in the lines so to speak, was never "who I was." I was creative, sensitive, and imaginative. I pondered deeply and always had this sense of "knowing." I never knew that the prophetic life was brewing in preparation early on.

For example: Dad would make a random inconsistent visit. I would experience unrest, anxiety, and a darkness that I could not explain when he would appear. Little did I know at that time he was struggling with a bi-polar disorder and alcoholism. Perception and discernment were gifts that were operative, though at the time I had no understanding, just emotional pain.

During my teens, I became enamored by the supernatural. Since I did not equate the supernatural with real Christianity, I sought it in other things. Ouija boards and experimentation with automatic handwriting, body levitation, and mind reading fascinated me. Fortunetellers seemed to have the same capacity to "know" things, and I embraced the excitement. I thought I had found my niche in life. My sister once reminded me that I would practice on her late at night. She was afraid of me because I could read her thoughts. All of this was done in innocence. I simply had no biblical understanding or revelation of a Holy God. So instead, I played in the pigpen of the occult and had limited successes.

Though I feared God, deep inside I knew my life was different and there was a grace upon me amidst the dark side. I also knew I had been set apart. Occasionally, I would see flashing visions of me speaking before groups of people. You see, we are set apart early on!

Prophetic giftedness unbridled in a not born-again believer can mask itself as many things. It is not a battle of who ultimately wins (God or Satan.) It is simply masked, distorted, and confusing until truth invades us, the veil is removed, and we receive cleansing.

Even to this day, I seek to maintain purity in my own heart. For I know hidden issues, unhealed wounds, and wrong motives can greatly distort our gift, and so, I have summarized this by stressing the importance of absolute surrender! It is my intent to release the reader to learn, love, appreciate, and accept what life brings and has been brought to his or her life. As individuals we are always in the process of "becoming."

I have learned to appreciate, understand, and accept my past. There were so many times I would ponder, question God, and seek to be free from my past demons. All of my life has been the making of a prophetic voice. We must accept grace to endure and grow amidst all the inner turmoil.

As I look back, God's favor has always surrounded my life. I was born into an Italian family with extended relatives who were loving, fun, prosperous, and giving. My mother struggled to provide for my siblings and me; but gratefully, there was such an outpouring from aunts, uncles, and grandparents that we always had abundance.

I always had a passion for the church. With a firm understanding of family morals and values, I entered the house of faith fully embracing Christian fellowship with open arms and cultivated healthy, Godly relationships. My mother always stressed "familia." When I entered the Kingdom, my life was centered on the church fellowship and the brethren prophets that loved the bride of Christ. I live and long for the maturity, wholeness, and success of the body for which Christ died.

EPHESIANS 4:11-16 (NKJV) "AND HE HIMSELF GAVE SOME
TO BE APOSTLES, SOME PROPHETS, SOME EVANGELISTS, AND
SOME PASTORS AND TEACHERS, FOR THE EQUIPPING OF THE
SAINTS FOR THE WORK OF MINISTRY, FOR THE EDIFYING OF
THE BODY OF CHRIST, TILL WE ALL COME TO THE UNITY OF
THE FAITH AND OF THE KNOWLEDGE OF THE SON OF GOD,
TO A PERFECT MAN, TO THE MEASURE OF THE STATURE OF
THE FULLNESS OF CHRIST; THAT WE SHOULD NO LONGER BE
CHILDREN, TOSSED TO AND FRO AND CARRIED ABOUT WITH
EVERY WIND OF DOCTRINE, BY THE TRICKERY OF MEN, IN
THE CUNNING CRAFTINESS OF DECEITFUL PLOTTING, BUT,
SPEAKING THE TRUTH IN LOVE, MAY GROW UP IN ALL THINGS
INTO HIM WHO IS THE HEAD - CHRIST - FROM WHOM THE
WHOLE BODY, JOINED AND KNIT TOGETHER BY WHAT EVERY
JOINT SUPPLIES, ACCORDING TO THE EFFECTIVE WORKING
BY WHICH EVERY PART DOES ITS SHARE, CAUSES GROWTH OF
THE BODY FOR THE EDIFYING OF ITSELF IN LOVE."

GALATIANS 4:19 (NKJV) "MY LITTLE CHILDREN, FOR WHOM I
LABOR IN BIRTH AGAIN UNTIL CHRIST IS FORMED IN YOU. IT
IS TO THIS END I ALSO LABOR."

In retrospect, little had changed in me the day I accepted Christ. My
newfound religion enabled me to forgive others, motivated me to
attend church, stop smoking, and cease from using foul language. Even
though little changed inside of me, I felt clean and loved life once again.
The work of the cross, however, was more "external." I changed the way
I dressed, acted more civil, and fell into the habit of treating Sunday as
the "Sabbath." I did not realize then that the Sabbath rest of God was a
dwelling place for every believer 24/7.

I will never forget the launching into power, praise, and abundance
that took place nine months after I received Christ. In July of 1982 a
friend of mine persuaded me to attend a Wednesday night service at a
large charismatic church in Long Island, New York. It was there that I
received my prayer language. Radical transformation took place and I
began to "see." My life as a Christian changed and flourished in a new,
fresh way. I was now a believer and advocate for speaking in tongues.

Bishop Bill Hamon recently wrote a book, *70 Reasons for Speaking in Tongues*. I personally would like to add one more making it 71 – speaking in tongues is the most important asset Ruth Mangiacapre beholds! I have prayed for many people over the years to receive this gift, for it is, next to salvation, the key to unlocking our prophetic destiny.

ACTS 2:4 (NKJV) "AND THEY WERE ALL FILLED WITH THE HOLY SPIRIT AND BEGAN TO SPEAK WITH OTHER TONGUES, AS THE SPIRIT GAVE THEM UTTERANCE."

WHO AM I?
~ THE CALL ~

As I developed a daily habit of speaking in my "heavenly language," revelation began to unfold, and there was a fresh new level of conversing with the Lord that brought clarity and direction into my life. To this day, I am a tongue talker and unashamed of it!

In January 1984, I experienced my first visitation from the Lord when my son Andrew was just six weeks old. As most infants do, he woke me every few hours to eat. However, this night was different. I sensed an intense sweet Holy Presence when I entered his room. As I rocked and fed my son, I felt my ears were attuning in a very unfamiliar way. A majestic conversation began to take place, and in an unspoken, familiar voice I heard, "I have called you. If you will say 'yes,' my favor will be upon your life."

Without really understanding or knowing what I was answering to, I said "Yes." I felt such joy! Holy fear and all the chaos in my life now made sense. Heaven met my earth. When I put Andrew back in his crib I was still basking in my encounter with the King. I excitedly opened my Bible to **Jeremiah 1**. Was I also called as a prophet to the nations? Me? Yes! The Lord said He had called me. But called to what? I did not dare ask, for the affirmation response was the important thing at hand.

Further confirmation came the following Sunday. As Jesus opened the scroll and it was written to **Isaiah 61**, "my" personal scroll opened to **Ephesians 4**, which states,

"HE GAVE SOME TO BE APOSTLES, PROPHETS..." ETC.,

All that I could see was PROPHET! It was as if the word was highlighted on the page. I knew in my spirit that I was called to be a Prophet. All the visions, dreams, and perceptions made sense for the first time. However, the responsibility and the "weightiness" of the call, and its seriousness have never left me. Grace is not only for salvation, but to stand against the pressure of the process. I've learned to cling to the cross and simply love the Lord with all my heart, soul, and mind.

I felt I needed further confirmation for the calling the Lord had spoken to me and began to seek it through everyone I knew. This was a mistake. Friends, church members, elders, pastors, and family looked puzzled when I announced, "I am called to the office of a prophet." I learned the hard way; let the fruit come forth in season, and you will not have to tell anyone!

However, one dear friend sought the Lord on my behalf, and spoke a word to me that I trusted. She said, "The Lord says 'yes,' but be careful, as lying spirits will come against you." I didn't even know what a lying spirit was, but I knew this person spent quality time with the Lord. So I appreciated her heart. She did not dismiss what I told her but sought the Lord on my behalf. She demonstrated "honor." I valued and trusted her as a person who loved God and who loved me! What a priceless gift; the gift of true friendship. When deceptive thoughts tried to torment me, I had ammunition! The word of my friend was to guard against them.

Throughout the years, I have to come to value the friends God has put in my life. Because "prophets" can be moody, misunderstood, and "quirky," the Lord has graced me with several long-term relationships. It has kept me balanced, accountable, and has been a great source of strength and encouragement. Upcoming prophetic voices need solid nurturing people in their lives. An understanding heart and a listening ear can do wonders when you have had a disturbing dream or a nonsensical vision. Do you have people in your life who value you? Cherish them; they are a gift from God.

At a *Women's Aglow* meeting in 1984, I received my first official word from a minister concerning my destiny. She spoke into my calling, my gifting, and the fact that I needed clarity. Interestingly enough, 28 years later, I would be ministering in her church preaching and prophesying! I have had several intermittent prophetic words over the years concerning my call, my vision, and the process; and I cherish every one of them. However, I stress this one point – I did not need anyone to tell or validate me because of the visitation from the Lord. I knew what I knew. When Heaven speaks it is settled on earth! When someone asks me if I think he/she is called to the office of a prophet (or any other office for that matter), I question it. If God called you, you know it! Prophets received their call face to face. For example,

JEREMIAH 1:4 "THE WORD OF THE LORD CAME TO ME..."

QUESTIONS TO PONDER:

CAN YOU RECALL A TIME WHEN THE LORD CALLED YOU?

WHAT DID HE REVEAL?

HAVE YOU PURSUED IT?

WHY, OR WHY NOT?

WATCHMEN

Ruth Mangiacapre

Watchmen, what do you see
In the night watch as you arise
And take your post
Hidden task, relentless fervor
Oh kingdom come!
Sleepy eyes take a backseat
So warrior, wrestle on.
The battle has been won, so stand your guard
To maintain victory.
Secret cries to overshadow defeat
Souls in the balance
Some blood, others strangers
Dreams release assignments
Burdens prod momentum
Loving Him
Enabling us
Weariness is not an option
An honor to stand
History makers we are!

WATCHMEN ON THE WALL

The prophetic ministry begins and ends with burden bearing. Watchfulness, intercession, and prayer begin with a passion for righteousness, holiness, and intimacy. My first launch into prophetic ministry did not begin with the gift of prophecy, but with a deep commitment to the prayer closet. I love prayer meetings, intercessory gatherings, and spirit-led prayer. God initiates true intercession. I responded to those nudges whether early morning or midnight.

Intercessors have the privilege of "standing in the gap." I found a new love for people, the Body of Christ, the lost, and the wounded. Heaven's perspective replaced my earthly thinking. I remember the time a demon-possessed man was babbling while crossing the street. He was obviously dirty, perhaps homeless, and/or a mental patient. I stopped my car and began to weep as if I were his mother! "Lord," I cried, "He is someone's son!" The aching in my own heart for so many other situations such as this was not human tears. I understood Jeremiah as the weeping prophet.

The prophetic journey will entail many stops along the way of hurt, heartache, and pain. One cannot separate intercession from the prophetic lifestyle. It is through this process that our own hearts become free of judgment, finger pointing, pride, and self-righteousness. Our hearts begin to only respond to the issues close to the heart of Jesus. Intercessors watch and pray. They listen and wait. The watchman duty no longer entails charging into the prayer closet as bulls in a china shop; but instead, patiently waiting as Heaven's receptors. Cease all striving and faithfully know He is God.

PSALM 46:10 (NIV) "BE STILL AND KNOW THAT I AM GOD."

As intercessors we begin to see that our eye gates are blessed, as well as our ears.

MATTHEW 13:16 (NIV) "BLESSED ARE YOUR EYES, BECAUSE THEY SEE, AND YOUR EARS BECAUSE THEY HEAR."

The first ten years of my walk with the Lord were solely and wholly committed to the ministry of intercession. As a young mom, I was confined to many hours in the home. I absolutely loved it. I would awaken each day with a burden to pray, and love for my "prayer chair." I took advantage of the countless hours I was homebound. As I would rock my son, I would envision that he was some lost sheep God put on my heart that day. I cared for and carried many saints in the spirit. It was "prophetic act training" as I turned the raising of my children into an understanding of what God's heart is for His children.

Monday nights were very special as well. A group of intercessors would meet every week for many years. We would carry the load in the Spirit for our church. It was commonplace for us to begin at seven in the evening and finish around eleven, perhaps midnight. A true watchman intercessor does not count time. It becomes a lifestyle. As intercessors, we would "see things," the good, the bad and the ugly. We were being trained in the ways of wisdom and discretion.

God drew several women from our church who had a passion to see God's destiny unfold for our growing church body. Holy Spirit taught us corporate intercession. He expanded our gifts of discernment and taught us to carry His burdens. It was an awesome experience as we began to see His hand move upon our beloved fellowship.

Unfortunately, there is a certain air of pride and self-righteousness that can surface in intercessors. Am I the only one who sees? Why are we the only ones with a burden? I would hear of others that spent their Monday nights watching random sit-coms or shopping. Inwardly, I just "knew" I was loved by God more because I sacrificed those nights being obedient and spiritual. Surely anyone who did not pray in the same manner as we did was considered carnal.

God began to chip away at the many layers of self-righteousness and judgments I carried. The process was so painful as a watchman, intercessor, and budding prophet. God was revealing what was left "unchecked." I was a Jezebel in the making. I still needed healing in the area of submission, pride, and manipulation. I would use my "giftedness" to control my children and husband. As I would see and discern "sin," I verbalized to my family how Holy Spirit was watching their lives and that God was not pleased. This season went on for a few years, until I fasted for their deliverance. Or so I thought. As I positioned myself on the floor to pray and intercede for them, Holy Spirit said to me, "You are full of self righteousness." Well that ended that! I realized that left unchecked, I had the seeds of Jezebel brewing inside me. Jezebel seeks to gain control of others, as we see in **1 Kings 19**. My family was cowering under my immaturity, pride, and self-righteousness. I was using my gift to manipulate them. I am so sorrowful at times thinking of the fear and intimidation tactics I used many years ago. My family is very forgiving, and we have all learned and have grown beyond that crazy season!

The prophetic intercessor is shaped by the compassion of the Lord. In this process of God allowing our hearts to break for His will to be executed on the earth, one must become tender, pliable, and broken. The crushing of the pride of our own heart unfolds. Eventually, we only know "Thy will be done." We have the awesome privilege of partnering with Holy Spirit to bring the Father's will to this desperate planet called Earth.

Matthew 6:9-13 - In this manner, therefore, pray:

OUR FATHER IN HEAVEN, HALLOWED BE YOUR NAME.
YOUR KINGDOM COME, YOUR WILL BE DONE,
ON EARTH AS IT IS IN HEAVEN.
GIVE US THIS DAY OUR DAILY BREAD,
AND FORGIVE US OUR DEBTS,
AS WE FORGIVE OUR DEBTORS.
AND DO NOT LEAD US INTO TEMPTATION,
BUT DELIVER US FROM THE EVIL ONE.
FOR YOURS IS THE KINGDOM,
AND THE POWER, AND THE GLORY FOREVER.
AMEN.

Unless we can transition from "seeing and knowing" to the birthing prayer, we remain ignorant as watchman. Gossip, tale bearing, and criticism have no place at prophetic prayer gatherings. May God's mercy abound!

We must mentor and work with prophetic intercessors and watchmen. They need the seasoned prophet and pastoral oversight to see fully the fruit of this foundational ministry and the alliance that is formed within prophetic intercessors that can make or break the church body. Together, each individual faces the wall with purpose, passion, purity, and commitment to uphold the leadership and vision of a local house. God's will shall prevail and conquer. However, if pride, wrong motivation, and gossip rear their ugly heads, tension and disunity becomes a venomous undercurrent.

Intercessors are a foundational powerhouse if submitted to the vision of the local body. The gap is calling out for true watchman. Our nation and beyond need the tears of such saints to water the ground with perseverance and to prepare the way for sons and daughters to arise!

QUESTIONS TO PONDER

WHERE IS MY FOCUS IN INTERCESSION?

AM I STILL SENSITIVE TO GOD'S BURDENS?

WHAT CAN I PRACTICALLY DO TO KEEP MYSELF ALIGNED
WITH HEAVEN'S PURPOSE?

The Gift

Early on, I valued the prophetic utterances I would hear in church. One lady in particular had an incredible, accurate, and powerful word every time the church doors were open. I remember telling the Lord that I coveted her gift. I would watch her interact with others after church. She had so much joy and things in her life seemed in order. Prophetic people live in a fish bowl. Others are always watching. When we speak for the Lord, we become targeted by the brethren to examine our fruit. And so she provoked me to live an uncompromising life. To this day, we are the closest of friends though miles separate us.

Over the years, this lady I will call "Sue" mentored me in the gift. We became very good friends. When I moved from New York to North Carolina, she and I wept. We thought we would never see each other again. How wrong we were! Sue and I are "soul mates" as David and Jonathan were. We have ministered together and awaited our ministries as they unfolded. Sue was a very important piece of my puzzle.

I will never forget my first public prophetic word. I could even tell you what I wore that day! We were attending a vibrant, growing, charismatic church; and I always sat in the front row. I never wanted to miss a thing. We had awesome worship, and the atmosphere was charged with the power and presence of Holy Spirit. I saw in the spirit that we were there for a very long service and that there would be an outpouring. My stomach was in "knots," and I knew if I did not proclaim what I saw I would burst. As I stood in front of the congregation the word went something like this, "Rend your heart, not your garments, seek ME with all your heart this day. Revival is at hand; it is even nigh at your door." Shaking, I sat down and realized I that I had just prophesied revival would happen that day! The whole service I sat sweating it out. This was my first public utterance so I was really biting my nails at this point. However, I saw what I saw. I knew what I knew. And yes, we did have an outpouring that day and left late in the afternoon. People were weeping, getting delivered and I was so happy! I had "arrived", so my immature mind thought. I was a "true prophet of the Lord." I just "knew" that the Prophet was known by the length and accuracy of the gift. And so I lived to prophesy. I loved to prophesy and placed all my eggs in the gift of prophecy basket. Paul states in

1 Corinthians 14:3 (NKJV) "But he who prophesies speaks edification and exhortation and comfort to men."

Paul is saying all may prophesy one by one, so that all man may be encouraged. How little did I know of the call and all it entailed way back when I gave my first public word. In my mind, it all centered around prophesying. Surely if you were called as a prophet you would have more than accuracy, length, and empowerment in words. While this is true in part, I had much to learn. Embracing the prophetic as a lifestyle of intimacy, brokenness, surrender, submission, and acquiring wisdom is the reality I came to know.

While I camped out on Sunday morning prophecy, God was about to wreck my world on the inside. My heart was getting ready to be exposed. We all have fasted (hopefully) for more power, greater anointing, and so forth. I learned that every fast would ultimately take me to the road of revelation of issues lurking in the corners and cobwebs of my own heart. A gift is a gift – freely given, not based on merit. Fruit must be cultivated.

In our *School of the Prophets* we activate the gift of prophecy as well as words of knowledge, wisdom, and so on. However, our school embraces being mentored in life and in character, all with the result of being whole, healed, powerful, and integral.

Matthew 7 tells us the "false prophets" are known by the fruit of the spirit, rather than perfection or accuracy in the delivery of the word. My own personal standard is to emphasize purity and accuracy. Purity of the heart begins with a holy encounter.

> 2 CORINTHIANS 3:18 (NASB) "BUT WE ALL, WITH UNVEILED FACE, BEHOLDING AS IN A MIRROR THE GLORY OF THE LORD, ARE BEING TRANSFORMED INTO THE SAME IMAGE FROM GLORY TO GLORY, JUST AS FROM THE LORD, THE SPIRIT."

As I mentored, trained, and activated countless believers in the gift of prophecy, I also spent an equal amount of time teaching on character and internal issues that can corrupt the gift. We must take responsibility for how we live our lives. At the same time, we are called to live a life of freedom. Holy Spirit trains, guides, and leads us. He alone convicts of sin. We also just recognize that we are the vessels the Spirit of God lives in. We are to speak truth, guidance, and necessary correction to those whom we equip. In addition, we must be willing to receive correction, too.

Ideally, our gift is received with gladness, as we not only express the "mind of God" and the will of God through prophetic utterances, but God's heart and character as well. We can then be assured our lives as prophetic people will be celebrated, and not just tolerated. There was a particular time in my life that I was really battling anxiety and fear. Although I was saved, it reared its ugly head again. Only now I was in full-time ministry as an Associate Pastor. I found that the intensity of my anxiety affected my ministry to others. Fear would grip my heart and the battleground to express the prophetic was intense. At one point I found I could no longer pray for people so I stepped back as I realized I needed healing and/or deliverance. The church paid for my airfare to fly to Ohio for intense ministry at

Restoring the Foundations. I came back healed. I am not saying you cannot minister if you are personally struggling, but it is wise to assess yourself from time to time and take the necessary steps to freedom.

Over the years, I have taught others that the prophetic words they speak will spring forth from a heart of love, mercy, and compassion, or bitterness, wounds, and hurts.

> JAMES 3:11 (NASB) "DOES A FOUNTAIN SEND OUT FROM THE SAME OPENING BOTH FRESH AND BITTER WATER?"

Ideally, the prophetic gift should be full of power, accuracy, revelation, sweetness, joy, love, and compassion. We are vessels of the Lord on a journey. Hopefully, we embrace growing in the fear of the Lord and so bring forth the fruit of righteousness. Words bring forth life or death. Words are weighty. They are not easily forgotten. The mere fact that prophecy is a vocal gift should challenge us to count the cost.

On a more positive note, I have seen countless hundreds of people be encouraged, healed, delivered, and restored as a result of people yielding themselves to being used in the prophetic gift. For example, there was a young man I knew who came to an "outpouring" service at our church one night. He seemed unsure of all that was happening around him. He had been raised in a solid Bible believing Baptist church, so our "river" style of worship and ministry was foreign to him. He trusted me, so I asked him if he would like personal ministry. He did not hesitate, but seemed a little reserved. I gathered a group of three that had gone through the *School of the Prophets* to speak words to him. Each one had a piece of his puzzle. One spoke to his destiny and calling, the other to his past and present situation (this brought faith to him that the prophetic is valid), and the last person addressed his need of freedom from the stronghold of drugs! He was broken that night as a direct result of the "gift." To this day he is free from addiction, attends our fellowship regularly, and has testified many times of the goodness of the Lord.

I tell our students that the prophetic gift is a gateway. It is a key that brings hope, healing, deliverance, purpose, and destiny to others. We must exercise the gift! Many people want dynamic prophesies full of words of knowledge and detail; yet there must be a starting place. Over the years, I have received the "more" because I exercised the gift. Continual use and practice brings the more and more.

ROMANS 12:6 "IF YOUR GIFT IS PROPHESYING, THEN PROPHESY IN ACCORDANCE WITH YOUR FAITH."

KEY POINTS IN GROWING IN YOUR GIFT:

1. Step out of the boat! I have found that most believers are not wrestling with the prophetic gift but rather the issues of faith. There comes a time where you will be "pushed overboard" or go willingly! **Romans 12:6** says we are to prophesy according to our faith.

2. All prophetic ministry must point to Jesus. Jesus is the Spirit of prophecy. It unveils his nature, character, and ways. Intimacy with the Lord produces words of life, hope, and healing.

3. Learn to listen, look, and sense. Daniel received great revelation and "more" when he looked into the vision. Pay attention to the Spirit. LOOK, LISTEN, SENSE! (**Daniel 7:13-14** and **Daniel 8:2-4**)

4. Glean wisdom from your pastor, mentor, and prophetic minister who can help you develop and grow.

5. Do not overlook the simple in search of the "more" or greater. Joni Ames tells of a story when her Pastor called her forward to give a word.

All she had was "Jesus loves you." She felt foolish giving such a simple word because anyone could do that! Her pride was at stake. However, she obeyed. A woman in the back of the church began sobbing and said, "I told the Lord this morning if someone did not tell me that God loved me, I would go home and commit suicide!" Obedience is key! Speak what you receive – no more, no less.

6. Boundaries for all! (**I Corinthians 14:3**) Edify to build. Exhort to provoke others to do the will of God. Comfort to relieve distress and despair.

7. Our prayer language is the greatest asset to grow in the gift. It transitions us from the realm of the natural into the spiritual. Exercise your prayer language on an ongoing, regular basis and you will be amazed at how easily prophetic revelation unfolds. As Peter preached in **Acts 2**, upon being baptized in the Holy Spirit, he reiterated Joel's prophecy, "Sons and daughters shall prophesy."

8. Intimacy is the key to knowing and understanding the heart of God and discerning the will of the Lord. Since the prophetic ministry is foretelling (futuristic) and forth telling (speaking forth the mind, heart, and will of God) how can one know the mind of the Lord without KNOWING GOD INTIMATELY?

9. Stay around faith builders. Dive into the Word! Learn to appreciate prophets. Sow into prophets and prophetic ministries with prayer and finances. The prophet's reward is the ability to see and hear. (**Matthew 10:41**)

10. Pay attention to dreams, visions, and perceptions. Test the spirits (**1 John 4:1**) Cultivate your gift by inquiring of the Lord when you are challenged, have questions, or just need wisdom.

ASK! ACTIVATE FAITH! LAUNCH OUT! READY, SET, GO!!!!

In 2003, I was with a team that went to Belize. We were on our "one day off;" and as a group, we decided that snorkeling would be great in such a popular resort area. I had always wanted to snorkel. It seemed easy and fun on the *Travel Channel*.

When the time came, it went something like this:

~ We had to pay $25.00 for equipment.
~ We were assigned a teacher. His name was Israel.
~ We took the boat out. I became very apprehensive as we left shore.
~ Storm clouds began to brew overhead. I became uneasy.
~ I put on my gear.
~ I froze as almost all my fellow missionaries jumped out of the boat and began snorkeling.
~ I never left the boat.

Lesson learned:

~ We each have a desire and a purpose.
~ We can be trained. I even paid the price.
~ We must leave the place of familiarity.
~ We must launch out in faith.

I realized that day many years ago that is the picture of so many of us.

FAITH IS THE LAUNCHING PAD!

THE KINGDOM IS AT HAND

We must make the conversion from the natural man to the spiritual man to walk in the fullness of prophetic ministry and truth. We must shift our mindsets in the prophetic. It is clearly stated in **Ephesians 4**, the mandate given to the Five Fold Ministry. Individuals are called to equip the saints for the work of the ministry. Prophets do not merely prophesy. It is so much more! The prophetic is used for edification, comfort, and exhortation. The purpose and value of "the gift" is to bring healing, motivation, vision, empowerment, and clarity to individuals so they may be released into their destiny.

Until we, as a people, fully understand the Kingdom of God being manifested on the earth, we are satisfied with living shallow, purposeless lives. Our aim will be living as nice people, perhaps raising nice children. Do-gooders become our standard. We need prophetic ministry to satisfy the empty places in our soul. To that end, a prophetic word ends with "self." Our future is severely limited to a very shallow, limited existence.

Let me make this clear. We do need wholeness, and the prophetic gateway enables us to be released from bondages and strongholds. We do need and desire to be faithful. Loving, kind Christians, and a good witness, do not necessarily shake the world. Only when we realize it is Christ in us, the hope of Glory displaying signs, wonders, and miracles, will the unsaved believe!

Prophetic ministry, understood and revered by those who have revelation of the Kingdom, releases the word of the Lord that will upset traditional thinking. Our passion for God's will to be done on earth as it is in Heaven, decrees and releases destiny over otherwise shallow, meaningless lives. The spoken word becomes the launching pad that releases power and momentum. A life without purpose can be transformed into a life that impacts the Kingdom of God. The kingdom of God is within us! Is it a reality? What is the Kingdom and how do we access it? **Matthew 16:19** says, "I have given you keys to the Kingdom,"

MATTHEW 6:9-13 (NASB) "OUR FATHER WHO IS IN HEAVEN, HALLOWED BE YOUR NAME. YOUR KINGDOM COME. YOUR WILL BE DONE, ON EARTH AS IT IS IN HEAVEN. GIVE US THIS DAY OUR DAILY BREAD. AND FORGIVE US OUR DEBTS, AS WE ALSO HAVE FORGIVEN OUR DEBTORS. AND DO NOT LEAD US INTO TEMPTATION, BUT DELIVER US FROM EVIL. FOR YOURS IS THE KINGDOM AND POWER AND THE GLORY FOREVER. AMEN."

A NEW PROPHETIC AUTHORITY

I found a new prophetic authority when I had full understanding of the "Kingdom of God." I found that God used me to release people into their destiny and impart faith through the prophetic word. When I first exercised the gift, it was all about relieving people from a current distress and giving them hope. It was a prophetic word embraced to help them cope while they waited to get to Heaven. The reality of Heaven is to be released through our earthen vessels. We walk in power and authority, and release it as we prophesy with understanding of the Kingdom. The prophetic is the gateway. It takes on a whole new dimension. Keys symbolize authority. We have the authority given by God to empower others to be used to establish His Kingdom on the earth. Our prophetic decrees help establish the Kingdom. As Myles Monroe states in *Kingdom Principles*, "*The Kingdom of Heaven is not a secret society."* It is ours when we enter the "Kingdom" through the doorway of salvation. Man's original purpose was to have "dominion over the earth." Dominion here is translated "manla kah" which is translated as "Kingdom." Dominion is the framework or boundary for our existence. The charge to have dominion over the earth raises the bar in prophetic ministry from temporal relief of our human pressure to motivate us to be used and functioning in our Kingdom purpose. What an awesome mind shift!

The prophetic charge is to establish, decree, declare, speak life, and release people to find their position in this Kingdom of God! When I first began to prophesy, God gave me a heart for the people. I was motivated to see people relieved of distress and bring the comfort. I camped at the comfort level for a very long time. I loved seeing people set free from pain, but found out many years later there was a holy agitation in me to prophesy at a higher level.

People of God are born for greatness. The prophetic is a key – a gateway to unlock destiny. Prophetic ministry, understood by those who have a heart for Kingdom purposes, becomes a powerful force to release people into Kingdom destiny.

I remember the day this concept became clear to me. I began to speak that if we were to dance, we would dance before nations; if we write, it would be read by the nations. Our counsel would minister wisdom to nations. I expanded my borders from personal (counseling) to counsel nations (Kingdom). Individual puzzle pieces are meaningless and useless without a revelation of the Kingdom on earth. Jeremiah was called to be a prophet to the nations, though he physically never went; it was Jeremiah's Kingdom mandate. Imagine prophetic voices covering the four corners of the earth.

I view every individual as a vital part of the Kingdom of God revealed on the earth. We must honor and value people as well as wholeheartedly love God, to aspire to this realm in the prophetic. **Philippians 2:3** states,

> "DO NOTHING FROM SELFISH AMBITION OR CONCEIT, BUT IN HUMILITY COUNT OTHERS MORE SIGNIFICANT THAN YOURSELVES."

Our natural "eye" sees people's struggles; thus, we prophesy from the realm of what is "seen." However, the unseen realm is more real to us who fix our eyes on things above. As we position ourselves as being seated in heavenly places, our very words become a force that can change our world. **Ephesians 2:6** says,

> "...AND RAISED US UP WITH HIM AND SEATED US IN HEAVENLY PLACES IN CHRIST JESUS."

We begin to prophesy from Heaven's perspective. And so, we must "see" from heavenly positioning.

Ezekiel 37 brings revelation to this. Ezekiel was posed a question by God. "Can these bones live?" Ezekiel had to ponder and evaluate what was being asked of him. He had to "shift" from his earthly perspective to Heaven's eye view. He prophesied beyond the valley. No longer did he gaze upon temporal states, but his prophetic words spoke to destiny. The ultimate fruit of prophesying Kingdom reality created an exceedingly great army.

THE KINGDOM PERSPECTIVE BECAME A SEED

How well I remember the season I prophesied to only the valley! All I could see was dry bones. The Lord would impart love, grace, and comfort to the recipient, and I longed to see Heaven's view. The Kingdom perspective became a seed within me. I challenge each individual to inquire of the Lord to water their seed, as well. This allows one to see more lasting results of prophesying from a whole new level.

I was given a prophecy many years ago by a very well respected woman of God. She addressed all the areas of giftedness and wisdom the Lord had given me. However, her final note erased all the "good" deposits. She said that I was not obedient to what God had entrusted me with. I was devastated. I was a fairly new believer who had a heart that only wanted to please God. "Was I disobedient?" Perhaps, but in only one small area. The Lord had been dealing with me concerning leaving a fellowship I had been in for years. I procrastinated because I worked at the church and loyalties were strong. This woman of God saw the valley of dry bones and reinforced it. I left that morning meeting crushed and shamed. Did she have a partial truth? Was it redeeming? No. It looked into a temporal, present state with no hope for redemption. I learned a great lesson in those early years. Peoples' lives are precious to God. Honoring and valuing them brings out the diamond in the rough and creates a platform for destiny which in turn sets God's Kingdom in motion.

We must ask God to lift our eyes from the earthen realm and look into the tomorrows that await us. This prophesying from and for the Kingdom sets our lives into powerful momentum. It is easy to see the bones in the valley. It requires no challenge. Just look around! We may bring comfort and mercy to those entrapped. Temporary relief is good. The Kingdom prophetic voice creates energy and empowerment to trust, and releases an individual from living a "nice" Christian life to one who changes the world.

We can transition our thinking by examining the scriptures that pertain to Kingdom living and meditating on the love of God. Believers speak on the love of God, but only those who "receive" His pure, holy, consuming love will be forever changed. Love humbles us, frees us, and thus we truly understand "inheritance."

Revelation of Kingdom living and living as a beloved son/daughter are an unstoppable force. Love never fails! Our prophetic authority comes from the Father, authorized by the Son, and enabled by Holy Spirit. Access the heavenlies by faith, grab hold of God's eye view, and see how God will transform your perspective. Your prophetic will cause Heaven to meet earth.

ᏝHE ᏝᎾURE ᎾᏝOICE

I have a standard in teaching prophetic ministry. It is to bring forth purity and accuracy. The need to set a standard is of utmost importance. Most people have no standard by which they measure their days. So day to day we drift. We wait for extreme changes to affect our lives, rather than set an attainable standard. I want to be a pure voice. I want my words to bring the reality of Heaven into focus.

Our God is a consuming fire. The fire of Pentecost should be an ever-present reality. Fire purifies us as we submit to the process. The sad reality is that we misconstrue the loving discipline of the Lord as demonic attacks, and we miss His great transformation process that only comes as we submit to the purging fire. There are great men and women of God who will tell you that the road to becoming "influential" comes at a great price. The great price is an internal upheaval. Old mindsets change. Heart issues become exposed. Emotional instability must experience death and resurrection. All unforgiveness and bitterness must encounter Truth. To the degree we desire purity in the prophetic, even the smallest of impure motives and hindrances must be dealt with. We learn to yield to mercy on our journey. Great grace enables us!

As a young girl, the gifts God place inside me became distorted. I spent a few years after high school on a quest to "examine" and play with the perceptive awareness. I found that mind reading became as easy to me as breathing. I believed that dabbling with the Ouija board and drugs (what a dangerous combination) enhanced my so called "gift." I also found handwriting analysis interesting and was told I was incredibly accurate. This was evil practice. It simply was fun and brought me an element of temporary fulfillment. I found if I thought hard enough with concentration and will power, anything could happen. I remember one night, in a basement on Long Island, New York, I conducted a levitation experiment with six other young ladies. Together we levitated a fairly overweight friend six inches off the floor! We never sensed that it was demonic. We were merely having fun. We would smoke marijuana to enhance all of our craziness. Had I known this was destructive, I would have run from it. Deep down, I had a fear of God due to my Catholic background.

In addition to the mess of dabbling with the occult, I was also in Freudian therapy; and hypnosis was a major part of my "treatment." Needless to say, when God invaded my life in 1980, the process of becoming whole and free was in its infant stage. As soon as I was baptized in Holy Spirit, the zeal of the Lord consumed my life and has remained with me all these past 30 years. For that I'm eternally grateful. The zeal allows me to "minister" from great passion. Although I was immature in many ways, I was called and chosen. The anointing was not dependent on my Biblical knowledge, nor "service time" in the kingdom.

As a result of Holy Spirit baptism, I quickly looked for ways to serve God. This led me to be a phone counselor for the *700 Club*. It seemed they would pass on all the severe cases to me - demonic oppression, suicide, and so forth. I soon realized I was under a dark, weighty cloud, which had been so familiar in my life. I never thought for a moment that I did not have to carry it. And so the director of the regional *700 Club* counseling center gave me a name of a woman who did deliverance ministry. Her name was also Ruth. Within days, I found myself on her couch being prayed for by her and another couple. This process lasted seven hours. I could not believe that there were so many dark, hidden places lurking inside me that needed to go to the cross! And so the process of sanctification began! **Isaiah 61** became my song. That night so long ago, discerning of spirits operated within me very strongly. My emphasis today is on the angelic rather than the demonic. Soon after that experience, I began to prophesy on a regular basis. The internal working out of sanctification was getting me in alignment with the outward minister in progress.

Throughout the years, I have witnessed many prophetically gifted people speak words of great depth and accuracy. They, however, missed one important aspect of the ministry.

> MATTHEW 7:16 (NASB) "YOU WILL KNOW THEM BY THEIR FRUITS. GRAPES ARE NOT GATHERED FROM THORN BUSHES NOR FIGS FROM THISTLES, ARE THEY?"

Some were markedly critical people who were judgmental and angry, and some were even rampant with sexual immorality. To that end, I have set personal standards. I set a goal to bring restoration to a ministry that is easily misunderstood and often rejected because giftedness exalts itself over character. It has become a very strong core value of mine; exemplify and be driven by the pure and holy love of God.

There were early years of prophesying very powerfully in church. However, before and after service times, tension and arguments filled my home. I remember experiencing a nagging sense that something was amiss. I remember all too well attempting to "apologize for my moodiness and outburst," simply because I wanted to "speak for the Lord" with a clean slate. My motivation was so wrong! I had to love and nurture my husband and children FIRST. My husband and children knew the hypocrisy I walked in behind closed doors.

I have come to appreciate the chastening of the Lord. New mercy every day! I tell students that the Lord still speaks through us, in spite of us. Many times God used me the most when my personal life and internal life was a mess! I had a standard, however, that would keep me focused. I placed greater value as Paul did on the formation of Christ on the inside.

GALATIANS 4:19 (NASB) "MY CHILDREN, WITH WHOM I AM AGAIN IN LABOR UNTIL CHRIST IS FORMED IN YOU."

PROCESS OF THE SEED (FROM SOP*)

The lifestyle of the emerging prophet can be compared to the parable of the seed. In agriculture, crop cultivation requires fertilized soil, water (from irrigation or rain) and seed. In the process of cultivation, the farmer is often required to initially till the land and control the weeds before ultimately harvesting the crop. The assessment of the land is crucial. (**Luke 8:5-18**) Crops can only thrive where that land has been broken. Brokenness simply means we allow the Spirit of God to uproot anger, lust, competition, jealousy, etc., so that we embrace true freedom, and thus minister with joy, love and compassion!

* 5 Runner School of the Prophets

The Summons

Elijah Task by John Sandford: *"The Christian is a watchman. His task upon the walls of the city claim him entirely. God acts in and through ALL that we are."*

There is an internal tension at work. This prods us to draw near to the very heart of God. We are to radiate passion and heart. We must not try to escape the chastening of the Lord.

> HEBREWS 12:6 (NIV) "BECAUSE THE LORD DISCIPLINES THE ONE HE LOVES, AND HE CHASTENS EVERYONE HE ACCEPTS AS HIS SON."

THE PARABLE OF THE SEED REVEALS THE SIGNIFICANCE OF THE SUMMONING PROCESS

Access your land! Identify your prophetic seed (dancer, prophetic artist, seer, teacher, healer, office gift of prophet, intercessor, etc.). What are your atmospheric conditions (your environment)?

Example: Faith or worrisome? Worshipful and peaceful? Are you positioning yourself to be tended to, and broken? Are there any underlying heart conditions (stony, bitter, grumbling)? Remember, out of the abundance of the heart the mouth speaks.

MATTHEW 12:34 (KJV) "... FOR OUT OF THE ABUNDANCE OF THE HEART THE MOUTH SPEAKETH."

I am learning the joy of living in the Glory. His presence is all I need. It liberates me from performance and it frees my heart from toiling. Yet I know that as I am becoming responsive to His Spirit on a continual basis, I am learning stewardship and responsibility. We "soak" because we are "sent." Some of my most powerful assignments were given as I lay on the floor soaking in glorious worship. In the process of abiding and loving Him, He lavishes great affliction and affirmation on us. When our hearts become His home, we are forever changed. **(Corinthians 3:18)** As we unveil ourselves, the Glory of the Lord purifies our hearts and allows our words to become and spring forth as pure, living water.

Prophetic purity and accuracy are the awesome fruit of learning to live a life of uninterrupted fellowship with God Himself. What an incredible and awesome God we serve! Can you recollect a time in your own personal life when you, too, were transformed in His presence? How? Sermons and preaching exhort us. Personal Bible study is necessary to reveal to us truth in life and living. However, one moment spent in His presence changes us for all eternity. The challenge we face in working with prophetic people is to convince them there is no secret to advancement. I simply convey that they must set a standard in the prophetic by subscribing to the principles:

1. Nestle close to the heart of God; YIELD to His love.
2. Become familiar with Holy Spirit.
3. Step out in faith.

> **HEBREWS 11:6 (NIV) "AND WITHOUT FAITH IT IS IMPOSSIBLE TO PLEASE GOD, BECAUSE ANYONE WHO COMES TO HIM MUST BELIEVE THAT HE EXISTS AND THAT HE REWARDS THOSE WHO EARNESTLY SEEK HIM."**

#

Ruth Mangiacapre

Have we not gleaned wisdom from those in flight?
Overhead, a delicate artwork of feathers and beaks
Sailing effortlessly to and fro,
Not anxiously in pursuit of a particular destination.
Just simply... Living in the moment
Wind driven
Briefly resting upon a higher plain,
Then gracefully a downward glide
Oh, how free!
Savoring each morsel of provision
Found along its travels.
Their song, so sweetly birthed in harmony with heaven
Never dependent upon atmospheric conditions
A parable given as a scroll for our own journey.

Seer or Nabi

In the third chapter of **1 Samuel**, we see a mentoring relationship between Eli, the priest, and Samuel. We can clearly see the simple dialogue and exchange of wisdom from Eli to the boy Samuel. When the Lord calls Samuel, Samuel assumed it was Eli because he had not been familiar with the voice of the Lord. After the Lord calls him a third time, Eli tells Samuel to go lie down, and says, "Speak Lord, Your servant is listening."

Such simplicity we can glean here:

1) Go posture yourself in an attitude of rest.
2) Tune your ears toward Heaven, and expect to hear Him speak!
3) LISTEN!

I have had the privilege of being coached and trained under some incredible men and women of God. Each stream as well as the people were uniquely different. Bishop Bill Hamon, with whom I hold credentials, is a Father of the prophetic movement. I would listen to his teaching and be motivated by the simplicity and faith he expressed in training the prophetic. Most *Christian International Prophets* I know are extremely accurate and powerful. The prophetic flow seemed fluent, powerful, and accurate. This really impressed me. I, too, longed for such a powerful, prophetic mantle. I could not get enough of the books and teachings Bishop Hamon released. Every prophetic word I personally received through a *Christian International* prophet was weighty and helped steer the course of my life and ministry. The impartation I received through Bishop Hamon's ministry was life altering. I also received great teaching from others as well. Steve Thompson of *Morningstar* confirmed my position to "train" and release when I first began teaching. The particular stream was easy, full of mercy, love, and good fruit (easy to be entreated). Joni Ames taught me that you could be yourself when you prophesy, and that the lives we touch are of great significance. Cindy Jacobs and James Goll imparted prophetic intercession. John and Paula Sandford were helpful on the process a prophet endures. There are so many of those that I am eternally grateful. Apostles Mike and Debbie Sirianni, my pastors, always encouraged me to set a standard and reach for it! Each of these people had their own unique style in the prophetic. In my training, I would learn the difference between the nabi prophet and the seer prophet. I am a seer, but I have learned to function as a nabi, as well.

Although the seer realm comes with greater ease, I actually have learned the nabi prophet is quite powerful. The Seer "to see". (**1 Samuel 9:9**) (**Isaiah 30:10**) (**1 Chronicles 29:29**)

THERE IS A CLEAR DISTINCTION BETWEEN THESE
TWO STREAMS OF THE PROPHETIC:

SEER = RA'AH + CHOZEH

RA'AH MEANS "TO SEE, GAZE UPON, TO LOOK, PERCEIVE
CHOZEH LITERALLY MEANS "A BEHOLDER OF A VISION"

John Paul Jackson notes, "*Seers are living parables. Their dreams, visions and speech patterns are filled with metaphors, analogies, and riddles that they do not even understand.*"

When I first began to understand the seer anointing, it helped me piece together and understand this realm of the prophetic. We are likened unto spiritual receptors (antennas.) At times we search tirelessly for the meaning of our dreams, visions, and perceptions, and fail at adequately communicating what we are discerning. Often, we ourselves do not understand. Very strong in discernment or spiritual intuition, the seer bears the weight of what is happening all around. Seers are hypersensitive to spiritual things; as well as, demonic strongholds and emotions. Seers tend to be deep, different, and even strange at times, as they have difficulty functioning in the natural realm. God uses this to chasten us as we learn and develop proper execution of prophetic ministry. Seers are always looking and soaring in the Spirit of God.

As a young seer prophet I thought ALL believers had dreams and visions, and ALL wrestled with demon spirits as I did in the night hour. I would share with anyone and everyone all of my spiritual experiences, including heavenly visitations. I retreated into a shell as I soon learned I was prone to error, spiritual pride, and the need to be more earthly good.

I became saddened that my Christian brothers and sisters did not understand me. I didn't know why. Who was I to turn to for guidance, mentorship, and growth? I never really feared being in error. Jesus always embraced me with His presence and I knew I was safe. I knew Holy Spirit as my teacher, guide, and truth Himself. I could not embrace fear, especially when God used me over many years to warn pastors and leaders of impending dangers. Much of this prophetic information came through dreams. Even to this day, there are very few nights that I do not dream. Some nights I dream four to five dreams, and I tend to get overwhelmed at the flood of revelation. I have learned to extract what is important in the "now" season.

IT IS OF THE UTMOST IMPORTANCE THAT PROPHETS JOURNAL THEIR DREAMS.

I have found that most dreams are symbolic and unfold over time. Steve Thompson states that dream interpretation is an art, not a science. Seers are strong watchmen and intercessors. Their keen ability to discern heavenly and demonic activity makes them very powerful vessels of God. They also warn shepherds of the onslaught of the attacks from the enemy. It is of great value to encourage seers to become enamored with the love of God and His Rule and Reign so that we have little time for second heaven warfare. Let's refocus and seek those things that are above.

DISCERNMENT

Discerning is a vital part of the life of the seer. A friend of mine equated the gift of discernment to peripheral vision. For example, suppose you were driving your car down the road, and a car pulled out from nowhere. Your peripheral vision would kick in. It protects us; however, we drive fixed on the road before us. We also do this in our walk with the Lord. We fix our eyes and focus on Jesus, the author and perfector of our faith, looking straight ahead. Imagine driving, turning from side to side! Many Christians walk as if they must always be on the lookout for the enemy. Jesus alone is our focus.

Discernment is a necessary and powerful gift given for protection. I choose to look and discern the activity of Heaven. Seers are receptors of the realm of the spirit. They absorb Heaven's revelation as sponges. Highly sensitive, they can be emotional and moody. Seers must aspire to maturity so they may use the seer gift with wisdom.

However, I have discerned that seers tend to be weaker in discerning the timing of the Lord. They may dream very powerfully, only to assume their revelation is imminent, when in actuality, years may pass before the unfolding of the dream or vision. Flighty seers seem unstable, even comical.

I moved to North Carolina in 1989; but in the mid-eighties, I had a dream in which I was speaking to a group of women and telling them, "I used to live in New York." It takes self-control and much needed restraint to weigh the information dreams and visions release.

One of the driving forces that led me to begin a school for upcoming prophetic ministries is to mentor them in the necessity of journaling, accountability, and sound advice. These practices will help fine-tune the seers' zeal and lack of understanding. I personally assume that unless there is an intense imminence of Heaven's information, there is wisdom in waiting. Usually, the interpretation of dreams unfolds over time. It is important to pray into every dream, tune into the realm of the spirit, and wait upon the Lord. Holy Spirit is such an incredible Teacher!

> JOHN 14:26 (NIV) "BUT THE ADVOCATE, THE HOLY SPIRIT, WHOM THE FATHER WILL SEND IN MY NAME, WILL TEACH YOU ALL THINGS AND WILL REMIND YOU OF EVERYTHING I HAVE SAID TO YOU."

I clearly remember 2:00 AM, September 11, 2001. I was in such a deep intense dream that I awoke in great alarm! In the most vivid and grueling experience, I was walking amongst body parts and smoke. I was "there" at the site as if it were actually happening. I awoke, ran downstairs and shook my husband as if I had seen a ghost! I said to him, "This is awful! Something awful is happening." The reality of that dream caused me to react immediately. Unfortunately, I did not respond in intercession, but in pure emotion. To this day, I have a heightened sense of urgency when the Lord gives solemn warning.

Since that fateful day in 2001, I am much more attentive to warning dreams. There have been several instances where I called upon intercessors to stand on the wall and sound the alarm against terrorism. I now decree peace over America! Homeland Security has done an incredible job averting disaster. I truly believe intercessors have been unleashing Heaven's strategy. For that purpose, we respond to watches of the night. Dreams protect and warn of impending danger. The seer needs to better understand the value of "dream language." God has purpose for everything under the heavens. (**Ecclesiastes 3:1**) God so graces seers with amazing sensitivity. Left unaccountable and without proper training and shepherding, they become over-emotional, disillusioned, and even bitter. Their receptors still are at work, yet they become overloaded with spiritual sensory stimulus. The response of the seer is to back down, shut off communication, or desperately try to find peace. However, the seer who seeks to gain wisdom, networks, and looks to enhance God's Kingdom, is a powerful protective force.

PERCEPTION

One must first learn to trust and value "perception." Perceive means to know by feelings. Perception is the simplest form of the seer realm. One grows in the separation of discerning the soul and the spirit. (**Hebrews 5:14**) Therefore, the necessity of inner healing greatly enhances this gift. Emotional wounds must be ultimately healed to enhance the ministry of perception.

Seers as children (not yet born again) are prone to confusion and fears as I was. The innate gift of the prophetic seer is in operation from birth. Although my parents hid their "differences" and rarely spoke of their poor marriage, I "knew" there was tension and darkness brooding in our home. Since I could not express my feelings or understand the atmospheric tension, I internalized their mess and became quite depressed. My father was bi-polar, an alcoholic, and a womanizer. In his presence, fear would grip me as I could sense he was about to run off again to his folly. If he was down, I was down. If he was aggressive, fear would overtake me. Many years of emotional trauma without understanding become locked up in the young life of a seer. Even as an adult, one must guard this precious gift. My husband and I have created an environment of peace, love, and worship in our home. Those who enter, whether believer or not, can sense our environment is peaceful and healthy. It is also a great opportunity to witness to others. For example, a lady came to visit with us and described her experience in our home as being easy and comfortable, like a big, soft recliner.

Seers are very strong in discernment. All prophets are seers, but not all seers are prophets. Seers are great intercessors, deliverers, poets, artists, writers, and musicians. Seers live in an alert and awakened realm of the spirit. They look, observe, see, and ponder. They spend much time inquiring of the Lord. This realm of the prophetic must be cultivated to reach full potential.

NABI

Nabi is a Hebrew word. It's root meaning is to bubble forth, as from a fountain, hence to utter. It is the first and most general term for a prophet. The prophet proclaims the message given to him. The seer "beheld the vision of God". **(Numbers 12:6-8)** The Old Testament prophet was the spokesman for God. He carried God's name and His authority. **(Exodus 7:1)** The seer receives, the nabi proclaims. Perhaps the clearest way to define the difference is that the Old Testament prophets would prophesy as the Spirit came upon them. It was momentary, fleeting. The unction propelled them to speak.

From the day of Pentecost, we see an internal work of Holy Spirit. The abiding power of God makes a huge difference in prophetic ministry. No longer must one wait till the God of Abraham, Isaac, and Jacob descends upon a man or woman and releases the message.

The New Testament prophet becomes the dwelling place of God. Holy Spirit individually creates a limitless supply of revelation and knowledge. We no longer live in waiting mode.

I have found most believers "wait" for the revelation to come to them. It is a readjustment in "thoughts" that a work is inside of them. **(John 1:1)** The word is Jesus; Jesus' nature, thoughts, aspirations, for us, His wisdom waiting to be released to change one's life. **(Revelation 19:11)** Jesus is the spirit of prophecy. The nabi "propheteia" means to bubble up, overflow, and flow forth life like a fountain. This is a new concept for those who only speak out a word when they see something. Prophetic people are always waiting for an absolute word. However, what pleases the Lord is stepping out in faith. Perfectionism creeps into this ministry and we can become performance oriented.

For many years, this bound me. I would wrestle with questions such as, "Is this a word for me? When should I deliver it? Will I look dumb? Will I stutter?" To make matters worse, my son told me I did stutter as I prophesied in church. The pressure of the prophetic put a lot of weight on me, since I had struggled most of my life with feelings of inadequacy.

I truly took on the Moses syndrome. "I can't" carried a great negative force in my own mind. I am now a "can do" person.

How did I conquer this? I realized that if I was ever going to fulfill my prophetic destiny, the only option was to move in faith. And so I began to speak more and more in faith. I would open my mouth and prophesy. It was much easier than the stress of holding back, waiting for a "download," or second guessing myself. Our very lives are preparation for the moments we prophesy and declare. There simply is no escape from a launch of faith. Peter had to step out of the boat. So why should we escape leaps of faith?

The nabi prophet has very little trouble with placing a demand on his or her gift. It is the seer that struggles because the very issue of catching Heaven and releasing it to earth carries a weight of responsibility. The seer needs time, discernment, and more understanding before delivering the word. They ponder, think, weigh it; and if they "discern" when the time is right, they will deliver the prophecy with such hesitancy.

The nabi does not wait. They move in faith, open up, then a well-spring pours out. A word goes forth. The nabi's word can seemingly be more dynamic, forthright, and charged with faith. Very rarely do they even recall their words with such proficiency as they see. The seer ponders more; the nabi simply delivers, speaks, and is finished.

I am a seer by nature. However, when I began to teach and train prophetic ministry, God thrust me into a seemingly long season of a nabi anointing and mantle. It was so that I would have been on both sides of the fence, so to speak, and be able to guide and relate with both. I am much more at ease as a seer. It is who I am. I must say, however, that nabi prophets carry more "weightiness." The words seem to be more power packed.

I have a friend who is a nabi prophet through and through. Very rarely does he dream. Visions are nearly non-existent and he will admit he has very little discernment. However, when he opens his mouth to prophesy, it is rich, detailed, and fluent; and the receiver has received a power packed, life-changing word.

When I challenge people to open their mouth and prophesy, it is foreign to them. It's foreign because, in part, I believe they have been given wrong teaching. Back in the 1980's when I was being discipled in spiritual gifts, I belonged to an incredible church on Long Island that both allowed prophecy, and also encouraged it. They believed in **1 Corinthians 14:31**. When it says *ALL*, that means every spirit-filled believer.

I soon realized that we were few in number. The liberty that I had experienced was foreign to most believers. I have met many along my journey who were gripped with fear. It was not a healthy fear of God, but a fear of making a mistake. Most commonly I would hear, "I am not going to give a word unless I KNOW it is from God," or that a false prophet was treated harshly and judged by God. So on and on....

So I looked into the Word to validate such a strict judgment. However, **Matthew 7** states,

> "A FALSE PROPHET IS KNOWN BY THE FRUIT THEY BRING FORTH."

This very chapter alone liberates those who strive for perfection. I do, however, hold a high standard for accuracy and purity. **John 5** sums it up for me,

> "ABIDE IN ME AND I IN YOU. APART FROM ME YOU CAN DO NOTHING."

If we only speak when we are one hundred percent sure, it eliminates the need to grow in faith, in confidence, and in reliance in God. The opposite is that we grow in self-confidence. I choose the former. If a prophet prophesies and his words do not come to pass, they are speaking presumptuously. We are not to fear them. (**Deuteronomy 18:22**)

There is no other five fold ministry that has such a demand on it for perfection as the prophetic. Pastors make mistakes, so do teachers, and so forth. But we should not be so flippant that we neglect standards of integrity and seek clarity. The fear of the Lord keeps you safe. (**Proverbs 29:25**)

A clearer understanding of grace is much needed. Remember, we are not Old Testament prophets of judgment where the messages were often harsh. We are New Testament people who have the abiding presence of Holy Spirit. And so we prophesy from grace and mercy. Let God's people, likewise, extend the same grace and mercy to God's mouthpieces.

And so, we have a somewhat clearer understanding of these two prophetic streams. In summary, the seer captures revelation, the nabi releases. Both are valued. Both, though different, show forth the diversity of gifts and callings.

OVERSHADOW ME

RUTH MANGIACAPRE

Hover

Breathe

Sing

Speak

Over me

Till my unformed substance gives birth

To my prophetic destiny

Is it part of your plan to let time escape

While this proclamation brews deep within?

Rally the intercessors, your hidden agents

The midwives to travail for me

This birth canal is where I am trapped

Yet there is no retreat for me.

Divine DNA is heavens choice

Grace will embrace His seed within.

ᎢHE ᎾNTERNAL ᏢROPHETIC ᏞIFE

Perhaps the most important part of our prophetic journey is the understanding that our internal life is of great value and significance to the quality of the prophetic we deliver.

Giftedness alone does not carry us through life's journey. The prophetic life begins and ends with the subtle internal tension of living a consecrated lifestyle. Holiness should never be imposed. A true revelation of the heart, mind, and character of the Godhead, sealed upon our hearts, changes us. We simply "become." Paul said in **Galatians 4:19** that he labored until Christ be formed in us. We all have a responsibility to represent Christ as He is – pure, kind, lovely, compassionate, full of truth and mercy. Anything else is religious jargon. And so, as we journey onward, God discloses hidden places in the heart – wounds that must be healed, attitudes that need to be adjusted, and carnal desires that need to be crucified.

For many years, I labored to be free. I saw myself in filth and hypocrisy, laboring to be free. Bible studies, deliverance ministry, inner healing sessions, and conferences and retreats became my game plan. For a while, I became more frustrated than free. I cannot recall when things changed. It was as if things became so much easier. Peace settled in me. I stopped the roller coaster and simply got off! I live now in a new, liberating way. I finally understood the Sabbath rest of God.

God began to unveil the inner secrets of His heart. He unveiled the motives of my heart, as well. It was sweet, not laborious nor fearful. The

God of Israel, Isaac, and Jacob touched those intimate places in my soul. As He did, my prophetic delivery changed. The more I allowed God's sweet presence to become my passion, the less emphasis I placed on ministering. Priorities changed. Prophecy is not something I do. It is who I am. Humbled by His love, chastened by His mercy, I learned to live out of **Micah 6:8 - 9 (NIV):**

> "HE HAS SHOWN YOU, O MORTAL, WHAT IS GOOD. AND WHAT DOES THE LORD REQUIRE OF YOU? TO ACT JUSTLY AND TO LOVE MERCY AND TO WALK HUMBLY WITH YOUR GOD."

ALL GENUINE PROPHETIC MINISTRY FLOWS FROM INTIMACY, HUMILITY, AND PASSION (COMPASSION)

Prior to this understanding, I ministered out of giftedness alone and my limited understanding of the Father's will.

Seasons come and seasons go. We in prophetic ministry are called to discern the seasons. I recognized that seasons of mourning, crying, and the dark night of the soul were tenderizing my hard and stubborn heart. Walls that had been erected by childhood trauma crumbled in the light of His presence. I now touched people and felt their pain, loneliness, and confusion. I longed to see people liberated and joyful again; so, I sought God for destiny-producing words for them.

There are many prophetic voices. There are few with prophetic hearts. Jeremiah was known as the "weeping prophet." I believe that his heart was wholeheartedly surrendered to God. His pure display of raw honesty clearly was self-doubt, anger, and hatred that prepared the way for a grace encounter. Grace, honesty, and humility are the key ingredients of a surrendered heart. God gives grace to the humble. Jeremiah wept over unfaithful Israel because of the tenderness and pliability of his heart. God wept through Jeremiah. He earned the prophetic mantle because he had an encounter with grace. God rejects our excuses for not fulfilling His mandate, as He did over Moses' will. Oh, the enabling power of Grace! And so the prophetic journey takes its protégé on a path of learning and growing into the ways and heart of God. Frustration rears its head as we try to understand the dealings of God.

Many years ago, soon after I received my call, our little family was thrust into financial problems. I had two small children and a husband who was bored in his job. He decided he would take his early pension and open a business. As much as I enjoyed the security of a union job and all its benefits, I stood behind his decision. Neither he nor I were prepared for the year ahead.

With virtually no savings account and four mouths to feed while building a business, we were thrust into a "faith" boot camp. Fears rose up in me that I thought I'd been delivered from. We literally had NO income. All monies had to be put into our small body shop for it to grow. I clearly remember standing in my kitchen. I had no food in the refrigerator, my car was out of commission, and I had no diapers for my two-year old. I held my Bible up to the heavens and angrily spoke, "God, you failed your word!" Then I threw the Bible on the floor. I heard an audible voice clearly in my spirit, "Ruth, if you can't believe me for the natural, you will never believe me for the supernatural."

WE WANT TO RAISE THE DEAD, YET COMPLAIN
WHEN WE HAVE LACK IN THE PANTRY!

This season became my training ground for the gift of faith. It was a season of lack, fear, and loss of control. However, as I look back upon that time, I would never exchange that year for anything. I literally saw miracle after miracle in the coming months. Money would appear in sugar bowls and refrigerators. Cars were fixed free of charge, all bills were met. Christmas was overflowing with gifts. Every day was a surprise! God's goodness invaded my worries.

I often reflect where God truly thrust me into a realm of faith I had only read about. Literally only $900.00 of salary came through our hands that year. We never lost our home, nor declared bankruptcy. Our credit rating remained intact. We were determined to pay all our bills and pay them on time.

THESE WERE LESSONS TO BE GAINED FOR
THE PROPHETIC MANTLE. DO WHAT IS RIGHT!

Learning does not come easy. I learned to communicate and interact with the Lord in a whole new dimension of tears, honesty, and raw emotion. I felt His presence, cherished his embrace, and lost a love for the things of this world. His presence, His power, His purity, and His prophetic word were what I lived for. I remember one night embracing the headboard of the bed as if it were the Lord. Oh, how I needed his anointing in my life.

Many people fail to understand the training process of life. The prophetic journey is the process of the purification of motives, intentions, heart issues, attitudes, and judgments. We are simply becoming what God intended us to be. The journey is just as important as the destination, if not more so. Learn to love the journey! Let each day unfold Heaven's intention for you!

Our prophetic delivery is an indicator of how well we respond to the issues of life. Each prophetic person is unique and hand crafted by the master potter. This uniqueness is tempered by life's experiences. As we embrace this truth, it liberates us from competition and striving to be like someone else. God's love for each individual is constant and sure.

Our perspective of God surfaces during bleak days. For this reason, we need a radical love encounter. Some need a heart transplant. **Matthew 12:34** says that from the abundance of the heart the mouth speaks. Are our words seasoned with grace? Is there compassion in the delivery of our words?

There was a time when I was frustrated being an associate pastor. I did not know about putting boundaries around my time. One Sunday, I preached on King Jehoshaphat. I thought it was a powerful message. When the service ended, my son said, "Mom, you look different when you are angry!" Boy, what a sobering moment. Our words are weighty. They impart. Our attitudes though seemingly hidden, surface in surprising ways. I had preached from frustration and anger rather than from God's love.

God, in his care and mercy, allows us to be chastened. Not that we should spend unnecessary time digging up issues, for this is the working of Holy Spirit. Most prophets and prophetic ministers go through varied trials, seasons, and misunderstandings. A strong aspect of prophetic ministry is to discern the times and the seasons. (**1 Chronicles 12:32** ... sons of Issachar, men who understood the times and knew what Israel should do...)

When we come to a place of absolute trust and surrender, we realize all our seasons have their purpose in making us who we are.

JEREMIAH 17:7-8 (NIV) "BUT BLESSED IS THE ONE WHO TRUSTS IN THE LORD, WHOSE CONFIDENCE IS IN HIM. THEY WILL BE LIKE A TREE PLANTED BY THE WATER THAT SENDS OUT ITS ROOTS BY THE STREAM. IT DOES NOT FEAR WHEN HEAT COMES; ITS LEAVES ARE ALWAYS GREEN. IT HAS NO WORRIES IN A YEAR OF DROUGHT AND NEVER FAILS TO BEAR FRUIT."

Fruit comes forth in the desert. Learn to love the barren seasons. Faith and trust are being built. Prophets should have a high standard of displaying courage, excellence, and responsibility, as well as, compassion and mercy. Forged through fiery trials and life's unpredictability, we emerge tenacious, strong, and bold. Be unshakable!

Sadly, we lose many along the way because they could not withstand the pressure of the potter's wheel. (**Jeremiah 18:6**) The variations of seasons equip us, empower us, and teach us. Unfortunately, bitterness, frustration, impatience, and hurts invade our space. Shake off the dust and allow the master potter to mold you into a masterpiece of victory!

It is so important to connect with a prophetic ministry or community that understands the ways of the Spirit. Remember, there is always a work brewing on the inside of us. When it seems like we are losing our grip, we may have a prophetic message brewing on the inside. Hosea married a harlot as a prophetic sign that Christ is married to the backslider. His life spoke a message! Can you imagine his pain and confusion? Yet, the master invaded his temporal comfort zone for the sake of revealing his heart. Only such submission and absolute surrender to the purposes and plans of God in our lives give us the conquering spirit we must have to experience ultimate fulfillment in our lives. Unfortunately, many prophets get lost along the way. Perhaps we have not preferred one another above ourselves. (**Romans 12:10**) In our quest to find our place and develop our calling and destiny, we have failed to extend true fellowship to one another. Relationships need to be forged along our way. Mentorship, discipleship, accountability, and simple love and understanding can mean life to someone's dreams during times of testing and adversity.

The many years of preparation were made easier because of deep friendships and bonds that were formed along the way. Learn to be a faithful and trusted friend. Emerging prophetic voices need this.

We can provide wise counsel to someone who loses his or her sense of identity during the dark night of the soul. We simply cannot go at it alone. I value my true friends. They are there for me, as I am there for them. We speak life; we extend love; and, when needed, a Godly chastening word. Our vision can be muddled; thus, we need true godly fellowship to help us see clearly. We do not forsake our gathering, nor should we lose sight of our need for others, their gifts, their impartation, and their wisdom. There are many so-called "John the Baptists." They are misguided voices supposedly crying out in the wilderness. They misrepresent the prophetic in that they mask their need for deliverance from an orphan spirit by hiding behind isolationism, as if it were noble. Yes, God does call us out for a time of separation, fasting, etc.; and we must remember that we were given a voice, a message. The message is to be released to people. Our ability to interact with people is what makes the difference in how it is received.

AN AWESOME WORD DELIVERED BY A GRUMPY,
CRITICAL PERSON WILL SOON BE PUT ON THE SHELF.
ON THE OTHER END OF THE SPECTRUM,
A SIMPLE WORD DELIVERED WITH A HEART OF
LOVE AND GRACE WILL BE WELL RECEIVED.

ALLOW GOD TO PURGE YOU, REFINE YOU, AND HEAL YOU

Humble yourselves, prophets of God! Delight in his presence. Let encounters change your internal life. Be not so quick to emphasize your gift above all. A truly surrendered life will find favor with both God and man. Suppose your gifts were suddenly removed; who would you be? Is your identity in the Lord and in Him alone? Are you hidden in Christ? **(Colossians 3:3)**

A transformed mind and life that carries great grace in the prophetic is a powerful force on the earth!

$\mathcal{D}$ REAM $\mathcal{O}$ N

JOEL 2:28 (NIV) "AND AFTERWARD, I WILL POUR OUT MY SPIRIT ON ALL PEOPLE. YOUR SONS AND DAUGHTERS WILL PROPHESY, YOUR OLD MEN WILL DREAM DREAMS, YOUR YOUNG MEN WILL SEE VISIONS."

ACTS 2:17 "IN THE LAST DAYS, GOD SAYS, I WILL POUR OUT MY SPIRIT ON ALL PEOPLE. YOUR SONS AND DAUGHTERS WILL PROPHESY, YOUR YOUNG MEN WILL SEE VISIONS, YOUR OLD MEN WILL DREAM DREAMS."

Dreams and visions are increasing and intensifying. There was a time in my walk that an occasional dream was significant and meaningful. However, over the years, I have witnessed a sharp increase in my dream life. Today, there is hardly one night that I do not have at least one dream. Mostly, they are detailed and intense.

Early in my prophetic journey, my dreams were clearly words of knowledge. If I would dream someone was ill with the flu, I would call them and, sure enough, they would be sick. Or, another time, I would dream a baby boy was born to a friend; and it soon came to pass in real life. It was a great opportunity to pray for healing. Perhaps, the Lord knew I was too immature for the symbolism in the night hours; so, He spoke clearly in present day facts. As I grew in the Lord, I found that there was a shift in my dreams. No longer were they easy to discern but rather difficult. Clarity turned to abstract symbolism. I had to mature, and it was clear He wanted me to inquire of Himself and seek meaning. I wrote my dreams in a journal. Because I was too much of a "black and white" person, deciphering them was difficult for me, but I knew the importance of recording them for future reference. Flexibility and a quest for skillful interpretation became a new part of my journey. Most people buy dream books, as I did, that include symbolism, interpretation manuals, and so forth. These are helpful, but we cannot substitute them for what Holy Spirit teaches us.

Steve Thompson told me once, *"dream interpretation is not a science, it is an art."* Dreaming is part of the seer calling. Get used to it! Adjust your mindset. Dreams are very important. This is when God is able to bypass our soul, our emotions, and prejudices and speak purely into our spirits while we are at complete rest.

There were many years I had poor interpretations skills. Since my dreams were so detailed and vivid, I would get lost in each color, each piece of information, and each symbol to the neglect of the whole. I finally came up with a novel idea. Just ask God! I simply said, "Lord, give me the ability to interpret my dreams."

HERE ARE A FEW TIDBITS OF INFORMATION THE LORD GAVE ME:

1. Write down dreams first thing in the morning. As the day progresses, details are lost.

2. What is the overall theme? **Example:** Travel to a new city? Giving birth? Getting a new home? Etc.

3. Who are the players? Are they familiar to you?

4. How did the dream affect you?

THERE ARE MANY EXCELLENT RESOURCES AVAILABLE. HERE IS A LIST OF SOME HIGHLY RECOMMENDED ONES:

1. Jane Hamon (*Dreams and Visions, Understanding and Interpreting God's Messages to You*)
2. Jim Goll (*Dream Language*)
3. Adam Thompson and Adrian Beale (*The Divinity Code*)

Seers need to be accustomed to dreams as part of their calling. Our limited understanding of the revelatory realm can be frustrating at times. The challenge for us is to understand that dreams are a vital part of our walk with God and learning to discern the ways of the Spirit. Dreams are God's communication method in the night hour. Never undermine their significance. They are not a second-class means for God to speak to us.

Most dreams pertain to the dreamer. Many think that some dreams are demonic. While it is true the enemy can oppress in the night hour, it is rare. There was a time it seemed like the enemy invaded my sleep. When I look back now, God was warning me of a situation that needed to be exposed. A person who lived upstairs from us in an apartment building had some serious lust and perversion strongholds. He would project them and target me. God in his mercy exposed this situation. The example points to the need for us to heed all our dreams.

I have had dreams in regards to a deceased loved one that would break my heart. Emotions would flare up such as anger, jealousy, or even revenge. I needed healing in these areas and, although I ignored the dreams, God was reminding me to continue to seek wholeness. God often uses dreams as a way of healing.

It is important to realize the ministry of Holy Spirit is in continuous motion. Many years ago, I was at a luncheon sitting across from Bob Jones. I had had a very detailed dream concerning an alligator. I simply asked him for its meaning, in his sweet voice and with wise counsel he simply stated, *"What does that mean to you?"* He prodded me to seek my own interpretation! Dependency upon another stronger prophetic person will inhibit our own growth. Confirmation is important and some guidance is always needed along the way; however, it should never replace us pressing into God for interpretation and inquiry of the Lord. Remember that dreams are either literal or symbolic. As you become familiar with the ways and voice of Holy Spirit, you will also be able to decipher dreams more clearly.

THESE ARE TWO VARIATIONS OF DREAMS:

1. **SYMBOLIC** – The Thursday before 9/11, I had a dream in which there were alien aircraft flying over my home. I said, "Look what the aliens are doing. They are invading my territory." Also, my mom was on the other side of the woods behind our home and could not get home. When the terrorists attacked the World Trade Center that fateful day, my mom was in Boston at my brother's and could not travel back to North Carolina for a week from Logan Airport. *Interpretation:* Aliens were terrorists invading our nation. Mom was stuck at my brother's home in Boston during that time and her coming back home was delayed for two weeks.

2. **LITERAL** – I was bathing a blonde hair boy. Two years later, I gave birth to my son Andrew. He had blonde hair and blue eyes.

3. **LITERAL** – In the early 1980's I had a very vivid dream that I was speaking before a group of women telling them, "I used to live in New

York." In 1989 we moved form Long Island to North Carolina.

4. **SYMBOLIC** – I dreamed that there was a six foot green snake in my back yard. It tried to attack me, but instead, attacked my daughter. *Interpretation* – Six is the number of man. Green is envy. A person was very jealous of my staff position at our church. The Lord warned me, so I did not react to the manipulation. My daughter was perceived to be a threat to this person's son, as she was engaged to her son's best friend. In a carnal retaliation, this person tried to break them up by "counseling" my future son-in-law against the engagement. She could not "bite" me but attempted to attack my daughter.

I remember vividly the day the Lord gave me the interpretation regarding the snake. I was at a conference in Charlotte, North Carolina, where *Morningstar Ministries* had a dream interpretation tent. At the time, I was sort of stuck between a mainline denominational church and a "river" church. I had gone with a good friend who also happened to be the church secretary. As I stood in line sheepishly awaiting my turn, she called me. I said, "You are not going to believe what I am doing. I am in a "dream interpretation line!" We both laughed. We laughed because we had been somewhat ostracized for our overly charismatic and prophetic aspirations. In essence, I secretly hoped no one would find out that I was becoming a sold out prophetic stream believer. There was an element of fear, perhaps some shame, certainly intimidation that I would be "found out" for who I REALLY was! When my turn came, I was pleasantly surprised at the ease and depth, yet simplicity of the dream's meaning. It was confirmed to me what I knew in my spirit of that person. It also challenged me that I, too, could and needed to seek my own gift of this spiritual "skill."

It challenged me to rise above criticism in my pursuit of revelation and God's Glory. I chose to stand that day. I chose to be unashamed and bold in my pursuit of God. I would not settle for anything less. Dreams have always played a large role in my prophetic experience and they continue to do so to this day. God uses dreams as a means to overshadow our souls, to direct us when we need guidance, to heal us form wounds, and to train us in the many ways of His Spirit. To that I say, "Dream On!" Let us welcome this important aspect of the seer prophetic ministry.

ℛESCUED

Ruth Mangiacapre

Here I sit, withdrawn from life,
Nestled in unseen arms, ever so securely.

So far removed from the temporal pace,
That ultimately takes my wind

Keep me here to linger, just a while longer.
For I am in need of such a rich embrace
I fear may fade away.

I yearn to throw they keys away,
And remain in this divine cocoon
Can time stand still for me this day?
I hope it shall be so.

I've needed this refuge more than empty calories,
A balanced checkbook
Even a dear friends voice.

Have I allowed unholy demands to chisel at my soul?
Competing for my affections?

My jealous lover rescued me even from my own will,
To cave to human pressure

Had I known how famished and parched I was,
An earlier escape there would have been indeed.

Ever so grateful for mercy's rescue.

Who Am I?
~ DEFINING YOUR DESTINY ~

While many emerging prophetic ministers can see their gifts and callings, few are focused. Each step is a hit and miss. "Where do I go from this place? Is there a true mentor out there for me somewhere who can help me define and redefine my goals?" The journey can be peculiar, confusing, and frustrating if we fail to position ourselves under selfless leaders, good pastoral covering, and an ongoing fresh daily walk with the Lord.

Perhaps, all the years I aimlessly wandered through the dark night of my own soul prepared me to understand the Body of Christ's need for mentoring. I had only one advantage in those years of isolation. I grew in my absolute trust that God was able to complete the work that He had begun in me. (**Philippians 1:6**)

This is how we come to the drawing board of our destiny. Begin with "Who am I? Where can I go from here?" Before Nehemiah built the walls, he had to make an assessment. (**Nehemiah 2:13-16**) Each of us must make a personal assessment of our own life with God. There are too many variations of prophetic ministry, we must define who WE are in order to become fruitful, effective, and focused. This is the key to the development of our gift and calling.

Let's take a look at this simply in a natural scenario. A child is born into a family. He appears active, inquisitive, energetic, and curious. As he moves form infancy to toddlerhood, he shows more interest in observing rather than participating in groups. He does well with building blocks, and on and on. His family welcomes kindergarten, as he needs socialization. School is difficult; however, he excels in English and grammar. He struggles throughout junior and high school. Everyone, including the parents, try to find tutors, coach him into athletics and sports, but to no avail. College would most likely be a local two-year college, until he "finds himself." Would he ever excel and be a white-collar worker like dad? The boy's frustration grows as the years progress. One day a guidance counselor meets with him and tests him. The counselor concludes that he is a visual learner, has a great aptitude for building electronics and computers, etc. All of a sudden his weaknesses are overshadowed by his strength. His eyes light up. Inside he screams, "This is who I am! This is what interests me and what I always wanted to be – a jet mechanic, a computer programmer! Now I know what to do." The course of direction is set. He makes goals, plans, and is focused.

Does this story remind you of yourself? Do you go through each day as it comes, haphazardly or focused, intentionally or distracted? Until you define who you are, your destiny is yet hidden from your sight. This can be frustrating and constitute many bound church-goers who live out each Sunday service as a dutiful obligation, with no personal responsibility to make the Kingdom a reality on earth. Sadly, the church has fallen short in this area. The Ephesians model of the fivefold ministry's mandate to equip the church has been limited to "preaching," winning souls, filling pews, and growing in expanding in numbers. Our discipleship has been Bible study, Sunday school, and various topical studies. These are good, but we fail to move to the more effective realm of mentorship and activation.

Jesus was the greatest equipper, mentor, and activator that ever lived! His disciples were challenged to extreme discipleship. There was never any question as to whether they were ready for ministry. This discipleship "program" involved laying down their lives, as they knew it, to follow Jesus, listen to His wisdom, and simply believe. I often wonder what Jesus would think of our "training methods" today. Intelligence and good people skills are not the necessary criteria to serve the King of Glory. Brokenness, humility, passion, and simple childlike faith are.

We start out our journey with hope and anticipation. We do what is necessary to make preparation for our calling. We pay the price. We let others who have gone before us teach and encourage us. Then the moment finally comes. We can either take a leap of faith, or let fear grip our hearts and watch others advance and move onward with joy.

Recalling back to the Belize medical mission trip of 2004, we had that day to sight-see, and the team opted to go snorkeling. With the dark clouds brewing overhead and the water choppy, I sat in the boat gripped with fear. I watched others around me snorkel to their hearts' delight.

I often refer back to that day as a lesson to many in our Christian experience.

You see my dear ones, it is all about taking a leap of faith. No one can do it for you. I promise you that He will always be your biggest cheerleader. Purpose in your heart to fulfill your calling, no matter how dark the clouds seem, or how choppy the waters get. DO NOT be a bystander in this adventurous journey. Prophetic ministry is activated by faith!

On the other hand, Jesus thrust his disciples into healing and deliverance, and signs and wonders long before they even knew the Lord's prayer. They were on the front line, and giftedness, mantles, and calling rose to the surface. Paul states in **Ephesians 1:1,**

> "I, PAUL, AN APOSTLE NOT CALLED BY THE WILL OF MAN, BUT THE WILL OF GOD."

One can only claim such a bold statement when there is precise and defined identity.

When one KNOWS who they are and whose they are, only then can one devise a clear executed plan for their destination. Our spiritual success is not measured by striving, nor by performance, but by our confidence in the One who has called us and is faithful to grace our lives with decisiveness, and faithful and passionate determination to fulfill our God-given call.

Sadly, most only hope they live out their lives with purpose. God is so desiring maturity and responsibility in our lives as we understand **John 15**, the chapter on abiding.

We abide, soak, and worship as if there is not a harvest to be reaped, or we work tirelessly and are works-driven until burnout ensues. I always say we soak because we are a sent people. Faith without works is dead.

> JAMES 2:26 (KJV) "FOR AS THE BODY WITHOUT THE SPIRIT IS DEAD, SO FAITH WITHOUT WORKS IS DEAD ALSO."

It is of the utmost importance that we press into the wisdom of God as to our earthly assignment and thank Him that He will empower us to "become." Early on, I was satisfied with my role as an intercessor and a seer. God used me to warn pastors of upcoming dangers, as well as, to encourage and undergird them. As prophets, we cannot randomly warn and correct leadership without relationship and proven maturity. We can only come to such a role when we know our place, our calling, and humbly submit to leaders, as well as, God Himself. Jesus Himself, being God, had favor with both His Father and man.

I have learned the art of intercession as a way of life. I have always loved prayer, prayer meetings, and gathering of intercessors, etc. Because of my passion for the place of prayer, I was able to identify myself as an intercessor. Little did I realize back then that it was the very formational place for all prophets. As prophets, we can never leave the place of intercession. We learn how to stand in it. Being a "Watchman on the wall" is always our position.

From the foundation of intercession, our identity and/or purpose becomes a little clearer. What begins to be fruitful comes to the surface, and our motivation becomes greater. I found that, although I loved prayer, it birthed a new passion within me – to encourage leaders, stand with them, and fill in various gaps within the house of God. I was always at church, working in the nursery, cleaning, praying, and talking to visitors. I was becoming a pillar in the house of God. So much of the ministry God entrusted me with has been establishing a foundation in the house of God. I began to see myself as an arising prophetic voice called to establish works. (**Jeremiah 1:10**)

WHEN ONE CLEARLY KNOWS THEIR MISSION, IT IS A GREAT TIME SAVER

I did not get involved in "church activities" that would deviate from the mission at hand. It is easy to stay focused. As I began to see gifts and callings in others, it thrust me into teaching as well.

Back on Long Island, the churches were very charismatic in the early 1980's. Teaching and Bible study were the most emphasized ministries in church at that time. Yet, I also saw the need to teach others and help them grow in spiritual gifts. This led me to teaching workshops based on **1 Corinthians 12**. One must know their areas of strengths and weaknesses, as well. I so loved teaching and thrived in it. Whenever I held workshops, they were full; and people thrived on the teaching. But when I became overly zealous and attempted to "oversee" a Sunday school program, having to make last minute adjustments when volunteers were absent, I would become frustrated. Teaching and training were in my spiritual DNA, not administration over it!

A progression to speaking at retreats, conferences, and preaching were next on my journey. That season came fairly suddenly. I was on a mission trip to Panama in 1996, where they were holding a women's conference, and the pastor asked if I would preach during the Sunday morning service. I was excited and nervous at the same time. I preached my heart out. The pastor said he would have never guessed it was the first time I preached on a Sunday. He even took notes! I did not realize that the preparation had been compiling over many years as I matured prophetically.

One narrows down their identity in Christ over time. The progression went from intercession to encourager, to teacher, and from teacher to trainer. One never leaves their beginnings as they grow and expand. Intercessor is who I am – one who stand in the gap and discerns God's heart.

I am amazed at the number of people who have believed in Christ for many years and yet still do not know who they are in Christ, who Christ is in them, thus living their lives adrift, from church service to church service. Their dreams are an unattainable mountain. Frustration follows, and many are participating in some religious activity to pacify themselves.

WE HAVE BEEN GIVEN CHARGE
BY THE SPIRIT OF GOD TO FUNCTION
IN WHO HE HAS DESTINED US TO BE.

It is our responsibility to fulfill our purpose here on the earth. We are all members of one body, not having the same gifts or ministries. Our differences and abilities should make us love and depend more on one another, thus unifying us as one body. (**Romans 12:4-5**)

"Streamline" was the word of the Lord to me in 2011. Narrow your schedule to what is really in your calling. Do not add, nor take away. My strongest gifts are teaching, prophetic preaching, training, and intercession. So I stay within the boundaries of my God-given anointing and abilities. That is not to say I do not help nor serve. It simply means I am most fruitful and joyful when I am who I am! A dear pastor friend, Barbara Rispoli in New York, preached a message in which she spoke of identity. She stated, "I AM WHO I AM says I AM." That sums it up, doesn't it?

I was an associate pastor for 7 years. It was very uncomfortable for me to be constrained. I loved to travel. However, in that season God was refining me. He put a pastoral heart within me and I grew in mercy and compassion. I learned the art of listening to the Lord; and to people, as well. He stripped me of selfishness, and I honor the pastorate to this day. I believe they have the hardest job on the planet.

We need to learn to appreciate our seasons. Each one brings forth fruit, or prunes us. All stops are necessary along the way. We grow in wisdom, and we see our frail humanity. We depend on God to empower us to grow and become. So, the stopping places along the way each bring their challenges and victories. Each place helps define us, streamline us, and break us free from other's expectations.

And so I know who I am. I may not always know the future and what it holds, but I am able to make decisions based upon my identity. I am an intercessor, prophetic voice, preacher, discerner of seasons, and equipper and mentor. I work within the boundaries of my identity.

Who are you? Where are you most fruitful" Examine your journey. What brings you great joy? Where is your anointing and faith? Empowerment and momentum will be found in the confines of your identity.

Sit down. Take some time to make short-term goals, intermediate goals, and long-term goals. Do you have a mission/vision statement for your life? Find a coach, pastor, or friend who has vested interest in you to help you and hold you accountable. There is no excuse for us as children of God to miss our destiny. (**Habakkuk 2:2-3**)

Even now, this book is the materialization of what has been in my heart for years. Most writers wait for inspiration. And so I waited. I waited, and I waited some more. Nothing was happening until in January 2011; I decided I would tackle the book one day at a time. Each day, I made progress. It began with a vision, some thoughts, and goal setting. Each one of us can advance toward our destiny by making a decision to take action.

Prophetic people have limited themselves in many aspects. In our fear of having a "religious spirit," we shy away from a disciplined life-style. Our high and holy calling demands much flexibility and continual need for revelation. However, if we are to truly become world changers, a pure voice for the Kingdom, we need to draw upon the grace of God to accomplish tasks at hand.

Take a few moments and ponder on what the Lord has called you to do. Go away, get alone at all costs! Evaluate your impact and effect on the Kingdom. Can you change things? Schedules? Goals? Aspirations? Make decisions based upon your dreams!

KNOW WHO YOU ARE! KNOW YOUR MISSION! STREAMLINE, IF NECESSARY.

HERE ARE A FEW SUGGESTIONS:

1. Just as the world makes bucket lists of "things to do before you die" take a close, hard look at what God has put in your heart to do. Write it down.

2. Make a tangible, workable plan – one month, six months, five years, ten years. Tweak, as necessary, but keep moving forward.

3. Speak prophetic life and destiny over yourself daily! Purpose in your heart to be counted as the chosen, not just the called. (**1 Romans**)

HEAVENLY FATHER, EMPOWER THESE RISING
PROPHETIC VOICES, DREAMERS, SEERS,
AND WATCHMEN TO FINISH WELL!

REGARDLESS OF WHERE THEY HAVE
BEEN THUS FAR, GRACE THEM TO OVERCOME
ANY AND ALL HINDRANCES THAT ARE
STUMBLING BLOCKS.

HELP THEM TO ENJOY THE PROCESS OF
"BECOMING," YET FORGETTING WHAT LIES
BEHIND, THEY VALIANTLY MARCH FORWARD
WITH PRECISION, PURPOSE, VISION, AND JOY!
GREAT SHALL BE THEIR REWARD!

HOLY SPIRIT, PRECIOUS "PARACLETE" AND HELPER,
REMIND THEM THAT FINISHING WELL
IS WITHIN THEIR GRASP!

AMEN.

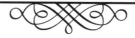

Thoughts

RUTH MANGIACAPRE

Some days the clouds seem like reality in this busy place
I can soar and weave in and out effortlessly
Oh how free!

My mind takes me to a distant land
Or back to the safety of my pillow
Shut eye

Night visions unfold.
Dreams fill the midnight hour.
Random, busy, real, productive, prophetic.
The alarm sounds!

Another day of thoughts
Some anxious, others sweet.
Many for sure!

Thoughts
They speak, invent, create, wander and yearn
A package of words

Pleasant scenes
A dark cloud tries to intervene
Amidst the beauty of this scene

Empty the clutter for another go round
Of heavens infused beauty!

Fly, expand, journey
Go for it!
Some take me to the higher place
Then dovetail to the valley.

What a gift!
This alphabet becomes the haven for the mind of God?

Cherish it, polish it, empty it , protect it,
Wrap it
In ink of liquid love.

BALANCE BETWEEN GRACE & TRUTH
~ THE WAY OF THE EAGLE ~

There is a tension in this hour for prophets to speak what people want to hear, rather than what is needed.

> PROVERBS 3:3 (NIV) "LET LOVE AND FAITHFULNESS NEVER LEAVE YOU, BIND THEM AROUND YOUR NECK, WRITE THEM ON THE TABLES OF YOUR HEART."

> JOHN 1:14 (NIV) "THE WORD BECAME FLESH AND MADE HIS DWELLING AMONG US. WE HAVE SEEN HIS GLORY, THE GLORY OF THE ONE AND ONLY SON, WHO CAME FROM THE FATHER, FULL OF GRACE AND TRUTH."

It seems that the prophetic ministry is either/or. We have yet to find the balance between grace and truth. We are either running around proclaiming "repent" or a Jesus who only doles out love and compassion, blanketing mercy to cover all transgressions. One would only hope that we have the tenacity and integrity to speak a sure, pure, whole word of the Lord.

> EPHESIANS 4:15 (NIV) "INSTEAD, SPEAKING THE TRUTH IN LOVE, WE WILL GROW TO BECOME IN EVERY RESPECT, THE MATURE BODY OF HIM WHO IS THE HEAD, THAT IS, CHRIST."

In **John 14:17,** Jesus called the Holy Spirit "the Spirit of Truth." Prophets seek truth. It is at the core of who they are. They have an innate supernatural ability to expose deception, fallacies, and half-truths. They settle for nothing less. They cry for balance, search for justice, and become uneasy around compromise. Their seriousness can be easily mistaken for pride or self-righteousness. Holiness screams from their being. Their quest for truth drives them relentlessly to seek the Father.

> PSALM 51:6 (KJV) "BEHOLD, THOU DESIREST TRUTH IN THE INWARD PARTS: AND IN THE HIDDEN PART THOU SHALT MAKE ME TO KNOW WISDOM."

This makes prophetic people strong in deliverance and inner healing. They look past what is obvious to the core issue at hand. Sometimes, people hide from prophetic people in unjust fear of exposure of secret sins, shame issues, and mistrust of ministry leaders because of dealing with untrained prophetic people in the past. I try to ease their issues by showing love and tenderness when revealing the heart of God to them. We need to love people to life using the prophetic words as a means to impart hope, healing, and restoration. The prophetic is a gateway, clear and simple.

We recently had a lady come through our teams for personal ministry; and although she came willingly on her own accord, she was obviously nervous. We assured her that the Lord was tender and merciful and full of compassion. We spoke into her destiny. She left in tears, joyful and healed. On her way out, she sheepishly asked if we would not tell her prophetic word to anyone. Confidences were very important to her. Apparently, she only knew prophets and prophetic minister to be invasive, harsh or judgmental. Many prophetic ministries only know Old Testament prophets as their example. They have not been trained to be full of New Testament mercy, kindness, and compassion. This new generation of arising voices will still speak truth, together with love. **(Ephesians 4:15)**

We are to deal kindly with all people, especially those of the household of faith. Few understand that only those in the prophetic office are charged to rebuke, correct, and give directional counsel. And so we have zealously gifted people, charging themselves to point fingers and judge lifestyles in an unfruitful manner. Without mentorship and training, we are like loose cannons waiting to go off anywhere and everywhere! Lord, help us to move in wisdom. Wisdom is supreme.

> PROVERBS 4:7 (KJV) "WISDOM IS THE PRINCIPAL THING; THEREFORE GET WISDOM: AND WITH ALL THY GETTING GET UNDERSTANDING."

I would ask for wisdom above giftedness. In my spirit I knew I would need to be wise as the Lord has entrusted me with a sphere of young prophetically gifted people. How many have the Word of the Lord without understanding His ways? If we look at the Master Prophet, Teacher, Jesus Himself, He was controlled, restrained, gentle, and truthful, as well. It would do us well to emulate the Great Teacher Himself. In confronting the woman at the well in **John 4**, it was a simple, truthful dialogue. We, as prophetic people, need to learn that dialogue, simple face-to-face confrontation with truth within the sweet boundaries of grace.

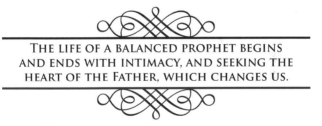

THE LIFE OF A BALANCED PROPHET BEGINS AND ENDS WITH INTIMACY, AND SEEKING THE HEART OF THE FATHER, WHICH CHANGES US.

Prior to that time, I was "bearing fruit;" I was very insightful and knowledgeable in the realm of the Spirit; and I let everyone know it, too, especially my family. I remember several incidences, which seem rather comical now. Before my husband was passionately serving the Lord, he loved the most ungodly heavy metal music. (I was very opinionated.) He walked in the door from work one day and the "spirit of rock music" was defiling my holy environment. I boldly proclaimed from the top of our stairs, "The Holy Spirit showed me exactly what you have been listening to!" We laugh about it today but that was a sampling of my prophetic outbursts of truth. I held my family hostage in more than one occasion by using my gift to control. Hmm! Does this sound like Miss Jezebel in the making?

There was a time I had a dream of some boys my son was befriending, of fairly serious potential trouble brewing. Instead of praying to gently warn him, I demanded that he find new friends because God spoke to me about it! He was only 12; and I imagine what he thought of an angry mom, and now, an angry God, too!

In another incident, my daughter called me from college, asking, "Has God showed you anything about me?" I replied, "No." She said, "Good, because I would have been embarrassed." Since that time, her walk with God has blossomed; and I am so proud of the Godly woman, wife, and mother she has become. It was obvious that because of my unchastened prophetic gift, all were held captive; or should I say, hostage, all because TRUTH greatly outweighed mercy. The reality is that mercy triumphs over judgment. (**James 2:13**)

As I began to grow in the grace and love of God, I swung the pendulum to err on the side of mercy. There were times I should have spoken with more authority. Perhaps my fear of man was never uprooted. Or it could have been that I tried so hard to "sugar coat" truth masquerading as "love."

There was a season I had to walk through as Associate Pastor where I was confronted by a very strong and aggressive Jezebel spirit. I knew not to handle it in my flesh. I was torn between anger and frustration, as the intimidating personality tried to undermine my authority. One day, she stood upright over my desk and boldly spoke to me, "I intimidate you, don't I?" At that surreal moment I had a choice to make. Prior to this point in time, I would have skirted this confrontation and said sheepishly, "Oh, no, you are not intimidating. I am sorry if I gave you that impression." However, truth rose up in me and I knew I was being empowered. I looked her dead in the eye and "Yes" came forth. She turned and walked away. I knew I could no longer skirt TRUTH in my inward parts. It disempowered the enemy. I gained victory that day.

People pleasing and prophetic anointing on an individual must be dealt with. Prophets are called to be courageous, bold, and honest. I encourage all of you to confront your inner demons head on. Allow the love of the Father to empower you to stand tall, face the giants in your land, and proclaim freedom!

IN THIS SEASON,
GOD IS RAISING UP A PROPHETIC VOICE
THAT IS PURE, FULL OF LOVE, AND GOOD FRUITS.

MATTHEW 7:16 (KJV) "YE SHALL KNOW THEM BY THEIR FRUITS."

Examine yourself in these areas. In speaking a word, whether corporately or individually, what is being heard? Love or anger, the heart of the Father or your own opinion?

To the degree we allow the mercy righteousness of God to penetrate our own brokenness, is the degree we will be heard and received. Remember, it is not just enough to be heard. (**1 Corinthians 13:1**)

Clanging cymbals do not alter the course of history!

ℰ𝒯ONGUES
~ OUR GATEWAY ~

As I look back upon my 30+ years operating in the prophetic ministry, I can see a definite correlation between my prayer language and prophesying. As a baby Christian, I was fortunate enough to belong to a church that was charismatic. I remember hearing a Fred Price teaching and his testimony of praying in the spirit at least 30 minutes a day. I am a person who likes boundaries, direction, and instruction. I believe it is important. Too many people in relationship with the Lord do not emphasize the need for discipline; I disagree. While there is plenty of room for grace and freedom, true godly discipline is formulated as the fruit of self-control takes hold. There is a strong need for responsible citizens in the Kingdom.

James 2:26b (NIV) says,

> "... SO FAITH WITHOUT DEEDS IS DEAD."

A simple but practical exercise in growing in the prophetic gift is to use your prayer language OFTEN! One cannot explain the correlation between the gift of tongues and the gift of the spirit, but the early church gained a power and momentum when they received this amazing gift! So are we to model our forerunners! Wake up with a song in your heart, tongues on your lips, and see how much spiritual seeing and knowing happens! Command your morning!

We must not fear sacrificing our freedom as "heirs" of the Kingdom to properly steward our gifts. It can be a cover-up for a slothful spirit!

(Ouch!) And so it would greatly enhance our relationship with Holy Spirit.

Jude 1:20 (NIV) speaks of,

> "BUILDING YOURSELVES UP IN YOUR MOST HOLY FAITH AND PRAYING IN THE HOLY SPIRIT."

How? Tongues, of course. It is the great connector to rise above the soulish realm and soar in the Spirit. Bishop Bill Hamon wrote a book, *70 Reasons for Speaking in Tongues*. I highly recommend it as a must read. A "must read" has to become a "must practice!"

I have ministered to countless people over the years and walked them through simple prayers of faith until they got their prayer language. It is amazing to watch the transition from being a content, natural being to one who delights in soaring into the unknown realm of the Spirit. It is simply amazing!

I knew very little of the revelatory realm of the Spirit until I was baptized in the Holy Spirit. There are many references to the prophetic being poured out upon the church where they were baptized in the Spirit of God. The greatest gift given to the church is the baptism in the Holy Spirit. **Jude 1:20** tells us to pray in the Spirit to build ourselves up! I begin almost all of my activations with my prayer language. I heard a dear friend and prophet, Martha Hester, tell us, "prophesying should be as easy as speaking in tongues."

There are diverse tongues – tongues known on the earth, languages found somewhere on the globe, and there are angelic tongues. Nothing will break a hard atmosphere like praying in the Spirit. I knew a lady who worked in her office during the day, and made it a habit of "thinking" in her prayer language! I have tried it, too, and it works!

Tongues of fire resting upon the disciples during the first outpouring, is a beautiful picture of the beginning of church history. Whenever I minister to a new believer, I try and envision tongues of fire descending upon them. Quickly, we need to impart such an awesome gift. Tongues and prophecy are like bread and butter; they simply go together.

*B*OUNDARIES

God established boundaries in **Genesis** when he proclaimed the "do not eat" statement. God set the world in order, every star in the sky, the sun, earth, and moon. The perfect balance and harmony. Order. Precision. Boundaries. Government. Rulership. Kingdom authority. Should we begin to examine the case for such boundaries around prophetic ministry as well?

My pastor, Mike Sirianni, is extremely gracious and trustworthy in releasing all ministry in our church. There came a time when we realized that there must be Biblical order implemented. People need to feel "safe," protected, and secure. My pastor has much grace in allowing Holy Spirit to move, and people love our fellowship for that very reason. Pastor said, "I say yes for a long time, and then the minute I say no, that it's not permissible at this time, people leave because I am controlling."

I personally extend much grace to budding prophets, but according to the word of God:

> 1 CORINTHIANS 14:40 (NIV) "EVERYTHING SHOULD BE DONE IN A FITTING AND ORDERLY WAY."

> 1 JOHN 4:1 (NIV) "DEAR FRIENDS, DO NOT BELIEVE EVERY SPIRIT, BUT TEST THE SPIRITS TO SEE WHETHER THEY ARE FROM GOD, BECAUSE MANY FALSE PROPHETS HAVE GONE OUT INTO THE WORLD."

1 CORINTHIANS 14:29 (NIV) "TWO OR THREE PROPHETS SHOULD SPEAK, AND THE OTHERS SHOULD WEIGH CAREFULLY WHAT IS SAID."

BOUNDARIES ARE A MUST FOR ALL CONCERNED. THESE ARE A FEW I BELIEVE ARE CRUCIAL TO MAINTAIN PROPHETIC INTEGRITY:

1. Submit to your leadership. If they have certain boundaries in place, honor and respect them with a grateful heart.

2. Exhortation, edification, and comfort are the scriptural boundaries for our lives. Correction, direction, and rebuke should be left to leadership.

3. Take someone with you when ministering. Ideally, prophetic words should be recorded or written down in case there is a question as to what was said.

4. Ideally, ladies should not be ministering to men, and vice versa. Use wisdom and restraint. Bring someone of the opposite sex with you.

5. Refrain from using terms such as "you should, you must, you have to." You are putting the receiver under pressure to perform.

6. Consider it an honor to speak destiny, hope, and encouragement into someone's life. Smile, be yourself, and minister with joy and compassion.

7. Stay in the Word! Those rich in the Word have a well of life from which to draw as they prophesy.

8. Nothing can be of a greater asset in prophetic ministry than wisdom.

PROVERBS 4:7 (NKJV) "WISDOM IS THE PRINCIPLE THING; THEREFORE GET WISDOM. AND IN ALL YOUR GETTING, GET UNDERSTANDING."

ASK FOR WISDOM!

About asking – God has not left us without simplicity. He simply knocks; we respond. He sets up His Word, we choose to agree and align. So to grow and move in prophetic ministry, we simply ask. Inquire of the Lord. I would be amazed at people who could prophesy with great clarity, knowledge, and accuracy.

ℐt is 𝒲ritten

The majority of this book addresses how to mature in prophetic ministry, but I would be remiss if I did not let you, the reader, know that the real test of prophetic growth is found within the pages of the Bible. Although I stress the importance of seeking God for wisdom and revelation (**Proverbs chapters 2 through 7**), the very foundation for our faith is that we study to show ourselves approved, a worker that needs not to be ashamed, rightly dividing the word of truth. (**2 Timothy 2:15**)

I was very fortunate to come into my relationship with Jesus early in the 1980's. Teaching and discipleship was the focus in the church at that time. We memorized scripture, and attended all sorts of Bible studies from the Tabernacle of Moses to Old and New Testament survey, etc. I remember one teacher playing guitar as we sang the books of the New Testament to Ten Little Indians! I always valued the word of God. Although I had difficulty in retention of reading in school as a child, I would read and re-read scripture to let it sink in my brain as an adult.

One day in church, I was sharing with a friend that I wanted to study all the time to make sure that I understood all of the Bible. With her gentle wisdom, she said to me, "Ruth, it is not all that important that you memorize the Bible from A to Z. What IS important is that you live what you read!" And so from that point on, I would meditate on scripture and allow my life to reflect what I read. Now, I can spend a whole month on one word or one verse, ponder it, think about it, and let it dig deep into the recesses of my soul.

I have many Bibles, all different translations and many study tools and guides. I value reading the Bible more than Christian books. I do have several authors that minister to me, but I always come back to my good old Bible. Nothing can replace it – no, nothing!

I am a very simple person. I love simplicity. I think that the overall message is the love of God meshed and hidden within the context of the Bible. The Bible is so intentional on revealing the nature of God that many a scholar could miss it to intellectualize and argue its contents. I have seen Christians argue and debate verses and chapters in the word of God to prove their points, and yet, their lives were not a reflection of the heart of God. Jesus addressed hypocrites in the New Testament very often; I want to live what I preach and preach what I live. Do I fall short of the mark? Absolutely! But if I choose to represent Him well, His Holy Spirit will be at work in my heart to repent quickly, and move forward.

I have always loved biographical stories. My favorite books as a child were *The Miracle Worker*, by William Gibson, and Anne Frank's autobiography, *The Diary of Anne Frank*. I had a vivid imagination. I could get inside their lives and envision what their lives must have been like. I do the same with scripture. I love the people of the Bible. Hannah, Esther, Ruth, Deborah, Jeremiah, Hosea, and Paul are some of my favorites. I have learned that one good way to study the word of God is to think about what they must have endured. I imagine their lives as they traveled and spoke about God. I think about their passion, and even their shortcomings. Some people enjoy history, others poetry. The Bible is full of surprises, adventure, mystery, and yes, even comedy. Imagine the panic of the disciples when they thought they were sinking on the Sea of Galilee? It must have looked like some sort of slapstick comedy as grown men were wailing to be delivered when their deliverer was restful right next to them.

Everyone loves the Psalms. My mom, who did not like to read the Bible because she was a perfectionist and did not want to make any mistakes in her Bible study classes, always found comfort in Psalms and Proverbs, as most do. Does that make them any less loved by God because they do not have the same standard for Bible reading? No, of course not. They may, perhaps, miss out on some insight and revelation that is found in much of the minor prophets; but they, nonetheless, are encouraged by what they do read.

I have learned that people need to grow and become at their own pace. Of course, teachers, preachers, prophets, etc. should become students of the Word of God. Not because they need to compete or showcase knowledge, rather, because they are responsible to equip the saints. Motivation is everything. If you love the God of the Bible, you will be drawn to feed on fresh manna every day. The Bible is food and nourishment for our souls. Aspiring prophetic voices will only prophesy to the degree that the word of God is alive and rich inside of them. I always teach that our lives are like Joseph's storehouse. We can only give from the storehouse within us. Is your storehouse full or pitifully empty?

Jesus taught in parables. He wanted people to dig for revelation, not for the probable or logical answer. He was teaching people to live from the unseen realm. That is how I like to look at scripture. Dig deeper than what you read. Ask for wisdom and revelation.

Think, ponder, chew it over. There is so much more than what your eye can see!

QUESTIONS TO PONDER:

DO YOU VALUE THE WORD OF GOD?

WHAT IS YOUR FAVORITE BOOK OF THE BIBLE?

DO YOU HAVE A HUNGER FOR THE WORD OF GOD?
IF NOT, WHY?

HOLY SPIRIT,
TEACH ME TO LOVE AND VALUE YOUR WORD
IN A FRESH NEW WAY.
GRACE ME
WITH UNDERSTANDING AND REVELATION
IN THE KNOWLEDGE OF WHO YOU ARE.
LET THE GOD OF THE BIBLE REVEAL HIS HEART,
HIS NATURE, AND HIS PURPOSES TO ME.
REMOVE ALL HINDRANCES
AND DISTRACTION FROM MY LIFE
THAT INTERFERE
WITH MY QUIET AND MEDITATIVE TIME.
IN JESUS NAME,
AMEN!

ᏚHE ᏦEW ᏦRONTIER

God is raising up a dissatisfied prophetic army that longs to love the unloveable. The world is full of people, such as women who shop with their young children, the teen with hidden scars on their arms, or the incoherent alcoholic with street signs. Yes, we are hitting the streets! One can only aspire to minister to these forgotten ones with a burning heart of compassion for those for whom He died.

The days are gone when the word of the Lord is restricted to the inside of our churches.

Each and everyday we are thrust into our world with a unique opportunity to touch their brokenness. It took me a long while before I continually looked for opportunities to love people I did not know. These are not limited to the down and out, but the up and out, as well. Emptiness is not a financial status, but the condition of an empty soul.

If prophesying is releasing the heart and mind of the Lord, we can be creative in how we minister. These are some of the ways I have used my prophetic authority to love those whom I have never met before:

I was returning from Scotland on the airplane, and I asked a woman behind me if she had a son. She nodded yes. I then proceeded to ask if he was in medical school. He was, and then I shared with her about how he would be very successful and take care of many in the family.

She was so touched that she handed me a beautiful handmade bracelet from Uganda, where she was born. I am sure her trip the USA got off to an amazing start because a stranger on the plane took the time to be a vessel that God could use. I cannot say it is always easy, for there have been times I get so caught up in the busyness of my day, and I tend to get caught up in my own agenda.

Another occasion took me by surprise. I was in Las Vegas on a family reunion, and I was walking my grandson and niece through a casino to get them to the game room.

I was quickly approached by a complete stranger who begged me to listen to her. She immediately began to open her heart to me about being backslidden, saying she was ashamed of her behavior. She kept repeating the fact that she did not know why she was telling me this. I took her aside, and literally in the middle of slot machine heaven, walked her through deliverance. I was stunned that day. She must have recognized that the God in me would help her state of mind. I was able to give her a referral to a ministry in Los Angeles.

You see, I was not looking to minister that day, but the mercy of God toward her overshadowed my agenda.

Another example is when I took my prophetic class to a downtown area near my home in North Carolina on a treasure hunt. Treasure hunts are where we hunt for God's treasures, listening to the clues He gives us. One of our team members had prepared himself before we began by writing down a word of encouragement. He said he was looking for a green jeep to put the word on the windshield; and it would be a surprise to the driver, even though we would never see the fruit of our labors. After looking for a while, we found the jeep and felt great joy to simply place the word on the car and proceed back home.

BE CREATIVE!
THESE ARE SOME WAYS YOU MAY TOUCH YOUR WORLD, AND BE USED BY GOD IN THE MARKETPLACE:

1. Take a five dollar bill or more, and ask God whom you might bless in a drive through fast food lane.

2. Ask the Lord for a picture or vision of the person He would have you pray for on any given day.

3. If you are confined to your home, write a letter to your pastor, or send an e-mail to encourage or comfort someone.

4. A compliment goes a long way. Purpose to find someone to extend kindness to. Conversations in a supermarket can lead to prayer, comfort, or an encouraging word.

5. Take a break while shopping in a mall, and ask the Lord to show you someone to give a word to. I once wrote a word on a piece of paper and handed it to a man who was taking tickets from children for a carousel ride.

Many believers are gun shy, so start in small baby steps! You can do this!!!

Don't take yourself so seriously! Make it a fun part of your Christian experience.

The River

RUTH MANGIACAPRE

Oh, that this river would engulf me,

till I know nothing of its fierceness.

Drowning and consuming all the excesses of life.

For we enter the river on overload and the currents tear asunder.

Weights it cannot carry.

Once I feared this place of destruction,

Knowing death awaits me there.

Come enter these waters!

Bravely and without hesitation.

Prepare your tombstone, engrave it bold and colorful for all to see.

Therein lies pride, control and shame. We cannot recognize the name.

See the resurrection of a bold and valiant warrior!

She's unscathed by religious onlookers mocking the process.

Raging rivers purify, simplify and ultimately glorify

The maker of this substance we call Living Water.

An invitation beckons all who cannot endure SELF and its pitfalls.

Come – abandon what you held so dear,

Escape the nothingness we call our lives.

Journey to the deep, unknown.

The King of the Seas the earth and sky has treasures

Awaiting you've yet to see.

Kingdom knowledge, Truth and Love.

The King graces each visitor with a key to return at your own discretion.

There is no fee, but a divine exchange.

One earthen vessel for sonship.

Who can refuse such a royal invitation?

ℊLORY

I could not finish my story with yesterday's experiences. I thought my book was finished, but my adventure continued way beyond what I thought was a completed project.

The reality is that I have learned more about prophetic ministry the last few years than I did in the first 25 years of my journey with the Lord. I would be amiss if I did not let the readers peek into my season of experiencing the glorious wonders of heavenly experiences.

In 2007, the year I launched out into itinerant ministry, I aligned with a very powerful prophetic stream, *Christian International*, the organization with whom I hold ordination. The regional meetings were held quarterly, and I eagerly attended them to glean and to receive impartation. A divine connection was about to unfold one Monday in South Carolina that would forever change my walk with the Lord. I met Gary Brooks, who was on the board of governors of *Christian International*. He looked a lot like a guy my husband would hang out with. He was dressed in motorcycle duds and seemed like he was in some other realm when we met and talked. He began to weep at the testimony of what God was doing at the meetings he was hosting. I loved his heart of passion, and invited him to do a meeting at my home church in High Point. He was all about the presence of the Lord, and I thought I knew all about what that meant, too!

It was a July meeting on a Friday night that he came along with all of his paraphernalia. This included spikenard, a crown, various jewels, and an array of beautiful and colorful objects. He took great care and caution as he prepared to arrange the platform, as if he was setting a stage for a passion play. He opened up the meeting talking about he Glory of the Lord and the visit he took into Heaven which radically changed his life from being an anointed preacher/prophet to an undone lover of Jesus. I could relate, or so I thought, because Jesus was my life, too; and I loved His presence and cherished His Word. Gary played CDs which were different, but nonetheless, very beautiful and spontaneous. He encouraged us to sit, lay down, or do whatever we felt would be conducive to meditating on the Lord and being at rest. The new term was "soaking."

The night went on for hours, and many people could not handle the extensive worship time, so they began to exit. I was determined to wait until Jesus Himself manifested to me. At or around midnight, Gary arose from his prostrate position and began ministering to people. This prophetic ministry was different. He would look at the objects on stage as if each one was hand picked for the receiver. I was undone when he handed me a jar of spikenard, and I began to weep. The Spirit of the Lord overshadowed me, and I heard very little of what was said, but I knew there was an eternal deposit made within my heart and an impartation of a new level of intimacy would emerge from that experience. As I went to bed that evening, I pondered on all that had transpired. I had been a dreamer most of my life but that night, my dream took on a whole other dimension. I found myself swimming in a river that was so vast and so cleansing, that I awoke to an urgency to write about it. My pen became a powerful tool and the creative scribe emerged from within me.

The River

I read that poem within a month at a women's retreat, and we had a glorious time in His presence. People began to experience His Glory in a new and profound way. I had lunch with Gary that day and as we shared I realized that up to that point in time, I only knew ministering from the anointing and not from the Glory. Dependence on the anointing allowed me to minister and see people set free and receive healing, as well as, minister in the gifts of the Spirit. I found there was a new and better way that night – ministering from the realm of God's Glory. It is in this place, the very heavy weightiness of the Chabod, He Himself reveals the wonders of His Kingdom, and we become transformed into His image. (**2 Corinthians 3:7**) Ministry no longer drains us but refreshes us. His heart is released and the very nature and character of God is on display.

I have been to glorious places in the spirit of God. Some I may share one day, some are too personal at this time. I have found my personal Jacob's ladder, and I have come to realize that God is no respecter of persons. There are present day Ezekiels, John the Revelators, Daniels, and so on. There IS a door open in Heaven for those brave enough to enter and knock.

I was in the presence of the Lord one day and I laid down, about to drift to sleep, when I found myself on the crystal sea, seeing creatures that moved like fish swiftly to and fro. I was fascinated that I was given the privilege to see such a Holy place. The fish were the souls that were new to the kingdom. God soon revealed to me that Heaven is REAL. When we entered into our eternal life upon salvation, we were invited to live in a new place. Religion tells us to simply endure, but God rent the veil. We are invited to live in heavenly places. We choose. I welcome experiences. I have lived a life grounded in the word and I absolutely trust the Spirit of Truth to keep me from deception. Sometimes we hide behind our fear of deception as an excuse to be accepted by those who tread not beyond this natural existence.

Yes, I have seen the four living creatures. Yes, I have been to many nations in the spirit. My identity is still in the Glorious Son of God. We can judge our experiences by the fruit they produce. I am more in love with Jesus than ever before. I have more joy and I love people more than ever. Is this bad fruit? I think not. When we focus only on ministering to people and releasing people into their calling and destiny, we place a greater emphasis on achievement and performance. In the kingdom of God, all creation worships the King. The highest calling ever given to man is what the apostle Paul knew.

> PHILIPPIANS 3:10 (NASB) "THAT I MAY KNOW HIM AND THE POWER OF HIS RESURRECTION AND THE FELLOWSHIP OF HIS SUFFERING, BEING CONFORMED TO HIS DEATH.'

> HABAKKUK 2:14 (NASB) "FOR THE EARTH WILL BE FILLED WITH THE KNOWLEDGE OF THE GLORY OF THE LORD AS THE WATERS COVER THE SEA."

I live to KNOW Him, and make Him known. It is my life's purpose. We create a habitation for the Lord Himself. We realize that the prophetic word and prophetic ministry reveals the heart of God. We become humbled that the maker of Heaven and earth chooses to dwell in an earthen vessel. Jesus Christ is the Spirit of prophecy. We are to understand that our intention in developing and growing in the prophetic is to draw people into the very heart and presence of the Lord. With that as our intention, there will be no limitation as to how the Lord can use us.

The Apostle Paul longed to visit the church at Rome (**Romans 1:11**) to impart a spiritual gift to establish the Lordship of Jesus. He is the head of the Church and the chief Cornerstone. I so want the church to restore people, and this can only transpire as we allow the cleansing fire of Holy Spirit to deal with pride, self exaltation, and our need for affirmation. Love God. Love people. Simple? Yes, only as we position ourselves to receive the love of God and let His holiness heal all our hidden places of brokenness.

One of the places that Samuel had the school of the prophets was Ramah. It was at Ramah that the scripture tells us that Rachel wept for her children. It is the ultimate picture of the true maturation of this ministry. It is called mothering, fathering, and mentoring. We are not to display what the grace of God has entrusted us with as if we had the market on it. We must nurture and train others to release the next generation and beyond.

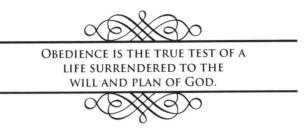

OBEDIENCE IS THE TRUE TEST OF A
LIFE SURRENDERED TO THE
WILL AND PLAN OF GOD.

It takes a heart of courage to make an impact on their world. I have been to many nations and cities. Most of the time, I knew why I was being sent; whether to preach, feed the children, or simply to accompany a team and do whatever the missionary needed. The joy I feel when I know I am being called somewhere by faith and not knowing the specifics is beyond words. It is like hidden treasure and Jesus guides and directs my steps.

Wherever I have been, whether to Spanish Harlem, or the Mayan Indian villages of Belize, intercession was the purpose. Prophet may be my mantle, but intercession is at the very core of whom I am. I have taken teams to the capital in Washington, D.C. and the ruins of the Twin Towers on an East Coast prophetic intercessory trip. When we were in Philadelphia, we prayed for the freedom to the city. Within 45 minutes of our leaving the city, a tornado ripped through the city. It was the first one in 35 years. I truly believe that when you walk in obedience even the land responds. Within days of our exiting Destin, Florida, a torrential rainstorm hit the region that had caused flooding and the closure of schools and businesses. We do have authority over the earth. Obedience is the key. Humility is empowerment knowing that HE directs our every move. To God alone belongs all Glory.

I consider it a joy to be a mouthpiece for the Lord in these last days, and my greatest pleasure is knowing that daily I walk, abide, and obey. Great grace is a surety as we live our lives for His pleasure.

As I close out this book, my *Prophetic Journey*, I write from the back seat of a trip to Germany. I knew only to come. It was not for big meetings, nor to preach and minister. Each day held a surprise. A conversation with a lost Italian lady whom we led to Jesus, a prayer for a broken foot, a word of encouragement to a guilt-ridden believer, a walk through age-old monasteries to receive an impartation that the early believers knew – simplicity of a walk with God. That is my life's message.

Yes, prophetic ministry and preaching to churches is the fulfillment of dreams I held dear to my heart for years. But there is so much more! The knowledge of the Glory of the Lord will cover the earth as the waters will cover the sea. And so I live to be an earthen vessel to carry the Glory of the Lord. As Heidi Baker said, "What does Glory look like?" It's simply looks like you and me, as we become one with the Father, Son, and Holy Spirit. (**John 17**)

What does your own prophetic journey speak of? It is uniquely yours. You have a voice to be heard. Incline your ear toward Heaven. Simply stand in the counsel of the Lord. Let others speak into your life. Live content and guard peace. Live in agreement with "it is written." Love the Lord with all your heart, soul, and mind and allow Him to love you and lavish His goodness on you. Be real, there are no limitations as to what God can do in and through a yielded life. Begin anew and afresh your own prophetic journey. Let the life of God touch the world through you!

I end this while sitting in a prayer center in Ulm, Germany. I had a desire from my youth to go to Germany one day. And here I am – fulfilling His plan for my life. Never underestimate the power of prophetic vision. Prophetic ministry begins and ends in communion with God – there is no greater place is our temporal existence. Heavenly experiences are simply another dimension of intimacy. Welcome all that the King of Glory purchased on that bloody cross so very long ago – so our lives would emanate His Glory across the earth.

You have a prophetic journey, too! Embrace the process. He is with you always, never leaves you nor forsakes you; and to that I say AMEN!

Made in the USA
Columbia, SC
30 July 2017